BRIGHT

THE TIN DRUM BY GÜNTER GRASS

Intelligent Education

INFLUENCE PUBLISHERS

Nashville, Tennessee

BRIGHT NOTES: The Tin Drum
www.BrightNotes.com

No part of this publication may be used or reproduced in any manner whatsoever without written permission, except in the case of brief quotations in critical articles and reviews. For permissions, contact Influence Publishers http://www.influencepublishers.com.

ISBN: 978-1-645421-76-4 (Paperback)
ISBN: 978-1-645421-77-1 (eBook)

Published in accordance with the U.S. Copyright Office Orphan Works and Mass Digitization report of the register of copyrights, June 2015.

Originally published by Monarch Press.
John D. Simons, 1974
2019 Edition published by Influence Publishers.

Interior design by Lapiz Digital Services. Cover Design by Thinkpen Designs.

Printed in the United States of America.

Library of Congress Cataloging-in-Publication Data forthcoming.
Names: Intelligent Education
Title: BRIGHT NOTES: The Tin Drum
Subject: STU004000 STUDY AIDS / Book Notes

CONTENTS

INTRODUCTION TO GÜNTER GRASS

NOTE TO THE STUDENT

Why does Oskar decide to remain three feet tall and to conceal his precocity? How does *The Tin Drum* serve as a **parody** of a classic work by Goethe? Why does Grass draw attention to the Virgin Mary's thigh? Why does he use a "wavering perspective" instead of a traditional "point of view"?

These are some of the many fascinating questions discussed in this Critical Commentary. It is designed to aid you in your study and appreciation of Grass' novel. But it will make little sense to you unless you are already familiar with the full text of *The Tin Drum* either in the original German or in the English translation. The author of this Critical Commentary assumes throughout his discussion that it will prompt you frequently to refer back to your original text.

The Editors

BIOGRAPHICAL SKETCH

Günter Wilhelm Grass, born October 16, 1927, in Danzig, is the son of middle-class merchants who spent his early years like most children attending school, playing in the streets, and going to the beach. Later in life Grass was to regard those early years of his life as the most formative because during that time he acquired the impressions, fears, and other sensations that determined the basis of his writing.

During the war he was a member of the Hitler Jugend (a Nazi youth organization), served with the military, and participated in the apocalyptic, final months of the war. Wounded in April, 1945, he was sent to a military hospital in Czechoslovakia arriving there a few days ahead of the American Army.

When he was released a year later with a full stomach and an empty pocket, he was confronted with the uncertain prospect of finding a way to support himself. Following a dissatisfying experience as a farm laborer, he was taken on at the potash mine near the town of Hildesheim. A belated effort to finish high school was quickly abandoned because the subject matter reminded him of feeding mentally on sawdust.

Grass decided to move to Dusseldorf where he could live with his sister while studying drawing and modeling at the art academy. While waiting for the school to open, he worked as an apprentice stonecutter in the firm Gobel und Moog. Later he joined two other impecunious friends to form a jazz band. In an early issue of Der Spiegel, Grass is shown accompanying his two friends on a washboard. The trio performed chiefly in potato cellars converted into night clubs.

The young man continued his studies in art and sculpture until his literary career began quite by accident in 1955. To be sure, he had always written poetry, but he never considered his efforts of sufficient quality to merit attention. The story goes that one day his wife Anna (whom he had married in 1954) took a poem from his desk and submitted it to a poetry contest sponsored by the South German Broadcasting Company. When his poem won third prize, Grass was introduced into influential literary circles and to new friends. About this time he managed to interest the publishing firm Luchterhand Verlag in his first book *Die Vorzuge der Windhuhner* (1956). Though the volume showed promise, it remained largely unnoticed.

With 300 Marks a month income from his publisher, Grass moved to Paris in 1956. While his wife studied dance, he worked on his first novel *The Tin Drum*. Two years later he was invited to read excerpts from his novel at the annual Gruppe '47 **convention** and so impressed the judges that he was awarded the 5000 Mark first prize. This event and the publication of the completed novel the following year brought the thirty-two year old author instant fame and financial independence. After the enormous success of *The Tin Drum* there followed in quick succession *Cat and Mouse* (1961), *Dog Years* (1963), a volume of lyrics, dramas, and short prose pieces. In 1969 the novel *Local Anaesthetic* appeared. His latest work, *Aus dem Tagebuch einer Schnecke* (1972) - roughly, *The Diary of a Snail*, has not yet been translated into English.

When the now-famous author received the Berlin Critics Prize in 1960, he left Paris for Berlin where he lives today with his wife and four children. To date, he has refused to buy not only a car, but even a television set and a telephone.

A liberal-minded intellectual, Grass feels he is dwelling in the land of the Philistines. He not only condemns present-day society as too materialistic but accuses his countrymen of being more occupied with the problems of buying a new car than with human rights. He never tires of portraying the average German as an overweight, undereducated bore perched upon a sturdy chair at a sidewalk cafe gobbling pastry and thinking about the evening's television programs. In an effort to awaken a sense of responsibility in his countrymen, he has devoted a great deal of his time to campaigning for Willy Brandt and his socialist party, the SPD (Sozialistische Partei Deutschlands). He has become a familiar sight during elections either making speeches for the SPD or handing out newspapers on the street. The party organizers at first discouraged him as much as possible, fearing his unorthodox methods would alienate more voters than he would attract. In the 1965 elections, for example, he designed his own campaign poster depicting a cock crowing Es-Pe-De (SPD). He then invited his audience to imagine the cock perched atop a dung heap rather than on the traditional church steeple.

Between campaigns Grass writes. Usually he works standing or leaning on a specially -built inclined writing-board affixed to the wall of his study. The author once described his manner of writing. It consists, he says, of three stages. In the first stage he writes down everything he wants to say in a roughly coherent fashion. This rough draft is made up of bits of experience, ideas, and personal sensations. In the second stage he expands the story with documentary material. Before writing Local Anaesthetic, for instance, he spent a good deal of time visiting mines and quarries to provide him with authentic background material. The third stage consists of polishing this material until the two parts fit smoothly together.

GRASS' THEMES AND TECHNIQUES

The Tin Drum must be placed among the most complex and intricately designed novels in world literature. As the book progresses, its complex structure, themes, and character development are revealed through several literary techniques. The novel's interrelated themes, its variety of characters, and especially the author's unique approach impress the reader that his work is another of those great artistic statements on man's situation in a complex world.

Grass' novel explores from many different angles what we may identify as:

Ten Major Themes

1. **Materialistic modern society has dehumanized the individual.**

2. **Our government, politics, and institutions are corrupt.**

3. **The individual as well as society has little if any effect on the course of history. Men are victims of an indifferent historical process used solely to achieve its ends.**

4. **The individual cannot avoid involvement in politics and history; nor can he deny personal responsibility for such involvement.**

5. **Objects possess an almost magical power that plays a significant role in determining man's thoughts, actions, and life.**

6. **Grass views the world in the manner of the Theater of the Absurd. Life is an activity without purpose, meaning, or unifying principle.**

7. **Both the rational and Christian interpretations of things are irrelevant to the true course of events.**

8. The unconscious mind is dominated by an all-consuming fear of the unknown.

9. God is dead.

10. All these conditions mean that there is a critical need for a New Messiah.

STRUCTURE

Grass uses the technique of free association to arrange his material. In the chapter "The Clothes Cupboard," for instance, we hear about a shiny patent-leather belt. Then the narrative spirals off on a series of related objects such as Oskar's experience on the breakwater with the eels, only to return a few pages later to the belt. Information and motifs introduced in the first two chapters may not reappear for several hundred pages while other motifs recur throughout the novel. Some symbols - such as white for innocence and crimson for transgression - will intrude upon our awareness again and again.

Another important structural element is time. The novel is not written chronologically, but actually begins in the present, reverts to the past, and then again to the present in constant, uncertain juxtaposition as Oskar narrates the events of his life.

Extended **Metaphor**: Although the traditional metaphor establishes a relationship between two unrelated objects, Grass treats the **metaphor** as an actual fact with no explanation as to its cause or meaning. In this way the dividing line between subject and object is erased. Such metaphors, highly imaginative, nonetheless influence the world of everyday reality. Thus Oskar's voice does, in reality, break windows, Niobe actually causes deaths, and the crowd on the parade ground really dances to Oskar's drum.

Parody: Grass is not a satirist, for he lacks the true satirist's optimistic belief that things can be put right in the world if we only set our minds to it. He is primarily a parodist. *The Tin Drum*, for example, is an extended **parody** of the Bildungsroman (*Novel of Education*) in which the development of the hero during his early years of immaturity and uncertainty to the maturation of his personality and capabilities is chronologically developed. During the course of the narrative, the hero is exposed to a wide spectrum of cultural influences, the theater, and especially to the influence of a spiritual mentor. It is through the pessimism of **parody** that Grass negates the optimistic view of life characteristic of this **genre**. Oskar's contact with the theater is limited to entertaining soldiers at the front with a troupe of touring midgets, his cultural influences are limited to those offered the proletarian milieu in Danzig-Langfuhr, and his spiritual mentor is the grotesque dwarf Bebra. In addition to the Bildungsroman, Grass parodies history, the picaresque novel, and contemporary events.

Point Of View: An author may choose to tell his story in either the first or third person. Although the first-person narrative allows the reader to empathize with the hero and move about inside his mind, it limits the reader's perspective strictly to one person. Third-person narrative, on the other hand, allows the storyteller to be everywhere at once, so the reader sees both the hero and other **protagonists** from many points of view. The versatile use of both techniques, however, creates yet a third device called wavering perspective. For instance, the reader is introduced to this last technique in the first chapter when Oskar insists that he is "in front of" the peephole while Bruno, his attendant, is "behind it." At other times he claims the opposite. This uncertainty of viewpoint is compounded by Oskar's frequent references to himself in the first person, then sometimes in the second. Frequently, the shifts occur in the same sentence. For instance, in the chapter, "Fizz Powder," Oskar says during his self-analysis: "Who was doing all this: Oskar, he, or I?" Such devices serve yet another purpose: alienation.

Narration As An Alienation Technique: The reader's uncertainty is created by this wavering perspective and the frequent shifts of narrative that inhibit the reader from empathizing with the hero. As a result, we are constantly held at arm's length and forced to look critically at both Oskar and the events he describes.

Literary, Cultural, Historical Parallels And Allusions: Grass uses many **allusions** to figures from mythology, folklore, and history as well as to other literary works to either universalize the situation or to create contrasts. Exploring various modes of self-scrutiny, Oskar identifies himself with Adam, Jonah, Tiny Tim, Jack the Giant Killer, Odysseus, Goethe, David, Abel, Jesus, Hamlet, Faust, Satan, Quasimodo, Yorick, Narses, and many others. Then there are direct **allusions** to the books of Dostoevsky, Goethe, and Melville as well as to the music of Wagner and Beethoven. In addition, cultural and religious references are made to The New Testament, Roman history, and the Gothic migrations.

Historical parallels abound. Grass invites us to see the similarity between recent history and the events of Oskar's life. The textual analysis that follows this section will provide us with many specific examples of this major device.

Sense Appeal: In his description, Grass constantly enlists the aid of our senses. In the chapter "Good Friday Fare," for example, because we can feel Anna's nausea we can empathize with her when she sees the longshoreman fishing for eels.

> **...the longshoreman extracted an enormous eel from the horse's ear, followed by a mess of white porridge from the horse's brain.**

Thus we are able to experience Anna's sensation of revulsion because Grass makes us feel what she feels, and we vomit with her:

> **...she disgorged her whole breakfast, pouring out lumpy egg white and threads of egg yolk mingled with lumps of bread soaked in cafe au lait over the stones of the breakwater.**

Humor and **Syntax**: Grass' humor especially results from his strong command of **syntax**. Much of his humor is achieved through parallel structure:

> **...Mama took me...on Thursday to share as it were her guilt, she led me on Saturday over cool and Catholic flagstones...**

Another device sets up an expectation...

> **Then there were the young doctors who were always chasing after the nurses and they wanted just one thing...**

which is immediately violated by an unexpected substitution:

> **...the nurses' cigarette stamps.**
> **The syntactical pun is used to good**

effect: Matzerath said "I do" in his Party uniform. Maria was in her third month.

Grass uses the non sequitur to achieve grotesque humor. For instance, when Roswitha is killed at the coffee machine, Oskar speculates:

But you couldn't see into your own heart, or else you'd have stayed with me instead of running after that coffee, which was much too hot.

Again, Oskar describes Schmuh's corpse after the car wreck:

Stiff and startled, he stared up at the sky, which was mostly cloudy.

THE TIN DRUM

. . . .

CHAPTER ONE: THE WIDE SKIRT

Title: The title refers to the four billowing skirts worn by Oskar's grandmother.

Narrative Technique: We might expect a novel that tells the story of Oskar Matzerath's life to begin in the past, proceed through digressions, characterizations, plots and subplots to a conclusion in the present. Günter Grass, however, eschews the traditional method of story-telling. Instead his technique resembles the way the mind works in recalling the past. Grass, claiming there is no distinct line dividing the present from the past, keeps the past and present always in constant juxtaposition while Oskar, the narrator, frequently switches from one to the other. As intended, this technique creates an atmosphere of doubt and uncertainty. It is, nevertheless, in accordance with reality since anyone's recollection of past experience is not chronological and is often mingled with the present. Accordingly, events that occurred recently (leaving only a superficial impression) are relegated to the back corners of the mind, while impressions which were made several years previously may remain more vivid than something that happened yesterday.

Point Of View: In establishing his wavering point of view, Oskar is pointing out that modern man cannot be viewed in traditional terms. Traditionally, authors have sought ways to equate the personal with the universal. Oskar claims that in the twentieth century, however, this is no longer possible. Consequently, he warns the reader against attempting to make a futile search for the transcendental truth, the archetypal image, and the metaphysical.

Insisting that his story will be an honest and straight forward narrative, Oskar proceeds to break his word almost immediately. While the account is honest, it is by no means straightforward. For instance, when he describes the peephole he says that the warden Bruno, an obtuse eccentric, keeps a constant watch through a peephole in the door. And yet Oskar refutes this by insisting he himself is sometimes in front of the peephole, sometimes behind it. This wavering perspective adds to the uncertainty and betrays the presence of the author behind the narrator. In this way he combines personal testimony with confession.

It is highly significant on which side of the peephole a person imagines himself. We usually assume that the person behind the peephole is not only doing the observing (and is therefore in a more secure position) but that he is also situated where he prefers to be. But when Oskar shifts the perspective and refers to himself as behind the hole, he reveals his attitude to his surroundings. Oskar tells us at the outset that he is a patient in a mental institution, committed there after a court trial. (The details are revealed only at the very end of the novel.) Yet he refers to his hospital room and his metal bed as the culmination of his life of struggle: his "final goal." Since Oskar assumes the role of observer, it follows that he must imagine himself behind the peephole.

In the first chapter there are several instances that indicate Oskar's satisfaction with his position. First, he receives visits from his lawyer and his friends, Klepp and Vittlar. These visits with the one-and-a-half hours of small talk and stilted pleasantries merely irritate Oskar and disturb his tranquility, although he exerts considerable effort to appear jovial. Oskar enjoys solitude, recounting an occasional story to Bruno, and most of all, his writing, which he refers to as excreting syllables on virgin paper.

Symbolism: The brief passage dealing with the five hundred sheets of paper is highly symbolic of Oskar's attitude to his own writing. Closely connected to the white color of his hospital bed is the whiteness of the writing paper. When he asks Bruno to acquire the paper for him, he stipulates that he should ask for unschuldiges paper... The English translation of unschuldig as virgin, however, does not adequately explain its ambiguous meaning. While unschuldig may sometimes mean virgin, it quite often means "guiltless." This translation more accurately renders the contextual meaning of the word, for the guiltless paper not only causes the guilty young female clerk to blush but it will also be soiled by the recounting of Oskar's black deeds. As the white of the paper is contrasted with the red blush of the sales girl, at the same time the symbolism of white for innocence and purity, red for transgression, is introduced. It is noteworthy that the drum is also red and white, thus heightening the dual nature of that instrument. These and other symbolic colors will occur frequently in the novel.

Theme And Characterization: The chief portion of the first chapter is devoted to the circumstances leading to the betrothal of Oskar's grandparents. With the artist's eye, Oskar pictures Anna Bronski roasting spuds on the edge of her potato field. From this pictorial description he shows how she is one with the earth. In fact, she blends in so well with the scenery that she is almost invisible. Oskar intensifies the **metaphor** by describing the way she sits on the ground as if grown into it, and later when she starts to stand up it is painful "as if she had grown roots."

The observations Anna makes watching the local gendarmes pursue Koljaiczek are seen from the viewpoint of her potatoes. Since her food comes from the potato field, it is therefore appropriate that whatever she sees is judged in relationship to the potato field. She perceives the vaudevillian spectacle that intrudes upon her field of vision as a series of visual impressions which she mentally arranges to fit into the familiar landscape. Here Oskar introduces the symbol of security and refuge of the four skirts that will recur throughout the novel. Anna Broski's skirts reveal how closely she lives to the earth. Each of them is of equal importance to her; each has the same potato-brown color with the same value. When the individual units are combined, however, they form a unified whole with each retaining its basic identity. Thus each skirt becomes subordinated to a definite system that enables Anna to establish coherence in her life. Even the days of the week are counted by which skirt is worn outside one day and moved to a new position the next. The most important days for Anna are those in which she busies herself with her wardrobe. Fridays the extra, fifth skirt is washed and hung out to dry, Saturday it is ironed, and Sunday it is worn to church. The fresh skirt is placed farthest from the body, while the one that is next to her body goes into the clothes hamper.

Yet the skirts assume another role: refuge. For instance, in the scene where Koljaiczek is pursued by the gendarmes, he hides under Anna's voluminous skirts while the minions of the law poke about in the fire and mice holes. Thus the skirts serve also as the family bedroom for it is under Anna's skirts that Oskar's mother and the future family are engendered. As a result, these skirts represent the source of life for Oskar. When later, as a child, he is permitted to creep under them, it is there that he is able to achieve a panoramic view of his family. He even regards these skirts as his true home, nostalgically remembering them at the top of the Eiffel tower during the second World War. Then again, toward the end of the novel when, pursued by the Black Witch, the escalator is about to deliver him into the hands of the police, he visualizes Anna Koljaiczek's skirts waiting at the top like a great mountain and wishes that he could slip under into eternal security. Thus, the skirts represent for him not only the origin of his existence but also the goal toward which he strives. He visualizes both a harmonious family life under them and regards the skirts as a place where all antithetical polarities are reconciled.

CHAPTER TWO: UNDER THE RAFT

Title: The title accurately summarizes the life and death of Grandfather Koljaiczek. He dies under a log raft trying to escape his German pursuers.

Theme And Characterization: When Joseph Koljaiczek leads his bride out of the potato fields and into the provincial capital, Oskar refuses to name the city at the mouth of the Mottlau until much later in order to focus the reader's attention on its central, administrative function. In doing so Oskar accurately reflects the Pomeranian, East Prussian agrarian attitude to cities, for towns and villages are not referred to by name but are considered only in reference to their economic, geographical, or political significance.

While the author pretends to tell the harmless story of Koljaiczek's life, in reality he is describing the eternal conflict between German and Pole, a conflict that had its beginnings with the invasion of the Teutonic Knights in the thirteenth century. Joseph Koljaiczek, a patriotic Pole, who has protested the partition of Poland by setting fire to German sawmills, becomes a different man when he tries to overcome his past and makes an attempt to adjust to the German's authority. By assuming the identity of a dead man, Wranka, he starts life over again. Having been married in both religious and civil ceremonies, he begins to live as a productive member of society. He earns his living by bringing large rafts of logs down to sawmills, he receives distinction as a soldier, and he joins the volunteer fire department. He even becomes a citizen of the German Empire. This picture of a well-ordered and peaceful existence, however, reflects only the superficial identity which Koljaiczek has assumed. Actually, the real Koljaiczek is just the opposite.

Nevertheless, Koljaiczek is not prepared to relinquish his new identity until forced to do so. It is on a trip upriver to buy timber that Duckerhoff, the new boss, comes aboard and recognizes Koljaiczek-Wranka. Although Duckerhoff says nothing, Koljaiczek concludes that his true identity has been discovered. Strangely enough, instead of escaping at the first opportunity, Koljaiczek is overcome by a bewildering inertia which proves to be his undoing.

The mounting tension between Duckerhoff and Koljaiczek is not projected by a traditional description but by dwelling on the military history of the region between Danzig and Kiev. This region is one that military strategists have regarded as admirably suited to war. Cleared and rolling, the countryside has the requisite number of hedgerows so that the maneuvers and showmanship jumping of the cavalry can be displayed.

Despite the opportunity to lament the sanguinary history of this region and the senseless suffering caused by innumerable wars, the author, by avoiding any moralizing leaves everything to the reader's imagination. Even Koljaiczek's paralyzing inertia is not explained, although it is clearly a reference to an unfortunate Polish tendency to trust their neighbors until it is too late.

When Duckerhoff informs the police of his suspicions after he returns to Danzig, with excruciating thoroughness the German Police launch a massive investigation into the identity of Wranka. Personally interviewing anyone who is remotely acquainted, they finally conclude that they have found the culprit who has eluded them for thirteen years. And so the police set out to capture Koljaiczek with their typical overkill. After the pursuit culminates in an absurd charade reminiscent of the Keystone Cops, Koljaiczek remains uncaptured. Seeking to escape, he dives under the raft and never surfaces. This incident gives rise to several legends, one of which reappears at significant points in the novel. It is said that Koljaiczek miraculously escaped and made his way to America, takes the name of Joe Colchic, lives in Buffalo, New York, and finally becomes a millionaire. It is in the pursuit and death of Joseph Koljaiczek that Grass reflects the German-Polish relations in all their ruthless inconclusiveness.

CHAPTER THREE: THE MOTH AND THE LIGHT BULB

Title: This chapter, named for the first thing Oskar sees after his birth, is symbolic as well as explanatory.

Historical Allusions: In describing his parents' betrothal and his own birth, Oskar employs the narrative method characteristic of the novel which we encountered in the first two chapters. Grass unfolds history against a backdrop of obscure, scurrilous, and proletarian biography that robs public events of dignity and reduces them to the simply trivial.

During World War I, Oskar's mother, Agnes, carries on a love affair with the Pole Jan Bronski. Although frail and shy, Jan is exceptionally handsome. Furthermore, he knows how to indulge Agnes' taste for luxuries. Despite Agnes' emotional attachment to Bronski, however, she makes a practical decision to marry the German Matzerath. In this and the following chapter, Oskar asks the reader to look for "cosmic references" in the Agnes-Matzerath-Bronski triangle by relating it to contemporary events. While Agnes manages the grocery store, the prosaic Matzerath officiates in the kitchen where he can metamorphosize his feelings into making the soup and washing the dishes. Shortly after the wedding, Agnes takes the quiet, passionate Bronski as her lover. This relationship parallels the arrangements made concerning Danzig after World War I. The significance of their wedding that takes place on the date of the Treaty of Rapallo, and Agnes' adultery on her wedding day, are amusing reflections of the fate of that treaty and a symbol of its failure.

Theme And Characterization: Oskar, who was born at the beginning of September, 1924, says he is one of those infants whose mental development is already complete at birth. He can hear, see, and think like an adult from the moment he is born. Grass means this attribute to be taken quite seriously, for it is not an excursion into the surreal.

It is at this early age that Oskar makes the choice that determines his life. He hears Matzerath promise that the grocery store will be his when he is grown, and his mother promising he will be given a tin drum when he is three.

Because Oskar takes an immediate dislike to Matzerath, whom he refuses to acknowledge as his father, it would appear that Oskar's mental development was indeed quite advanced even before his birth. It is not until later that we learn that Oskar regards Jan Bronski as his true father.

Oskar's interest in drums originates in the first few minutes of his life as he watches and listens to a moth, flown in through the window, that drums rhythmically against the light bulb. His reaction to the drumming sounds makes him decide to accept his mother's promise that she will give him a drum. Inasmuch as Oskar knows that his parents are not mentally equipped to understand his desire he decides to keep his adult intelligence a secret from them. Although this fact is by no means clearly stated, it is gradually implied as the events unfold.

At the end of this chapter, when Oskar first expresses his disillusionment with life and his desire to return to the womb, he establishes a **theme** that will be repeated often throughout the novel.

CHAPTER FOUR: THE PHOTOGRAPH ALBUM

Title: Shifting abruptly from past to present, Oskar recalls how he has hoarded an old photograph album which he brought with him to West Germany. Oskar uses this album, containing pictures from, the beginning of the century, as an organizing principle to link together the disparate parts of the novel.

Theme And Characterization: As Oskar compares himself to famous individuals in mythology and history who for one reason or another either could not or would not grow to full height, he decides to remain at the height of a three-year-old boy because this will exempt him from having to assume the role of an adult. Oskar knows that if he follows his father's plan he will one day take over the grocery store, get married, have children, and spend Sundays at grandmother's. He prefers to retain and develop his individuality unencumbered by social prescriptions and responsibilities. Thus by rejecting the achievement-oriented society, its work ethic, and its frantic consumerism, Oskar defies tradition.

Social **Satire**: Oskar believes that we can see the dehumanizing nature of modern society by considering the development of photography. Comparing a snapshot of Grandfather Koljaiczek with a recent passport photo of his friend Klepp, he notices a significant difference. While the picture of his grandfather is a small work of art, Klepp's photo appears to cry out for an official stamp. Without this notarization the photo appears incomplete. Photography can no longer be viewed as a means of giving pleasure but must be seen as a dehumanizing phenomenon of the modern age. Significantly, Oskar imagines Hell as a room where one is forced to look at modern snapshots for eternity.

Literary Technique: In a subtle comment on the modern novelistic technique, Oskar and Klepp spend one day a week cutting up snapshots. Then, they take the eyes, ears, noses, and mouths and paste them back together in grotesque mosaics.

When Grass was once asked why he does not use the straightforward narrative as he did for instance in Cat and Mouse, he replied that the absurd and the grotesque is the only suitable means for rendering reality in our present-day society.

Historical Allusions: In this chapter Grass makes one of his frequent historical allusions. Many of the photographs in his album were taken on excursions arranged by the Nazis in their

Strength-Through-Joy organization. Their many organizations were established to provide regimented leisure for the working class who could take vacations, attend sporting events, and patronize the theater at reduced rates.

CHAPTER FIVE: SMASH A LITTLE WINDOWPANE

Title: The original German title (Glas, Glas, Glaschen) is taken from a children's nonsense **rhyme**. The name of this chapter was chosen to explain Oskar's gift that enables him to shatter glass with his voice.

Theme: When Oskar decides not to grow, he realizes he must provide adults with some believable reason. So, accordingly, on his third birthday he arranges an accident. He falls down the cellar stairs and lands on his head, seriously injuring himself, exactly as he had planned.

Oskar's ability to shatter glass with his voice also dates from his third birthday. This ability is another of Grass' extended metaphors. It is presented without explanation and is meant to be taken at face value. Oskar likens his voice to a "chaste and merciless diamond" which can break vases, demolish windowpanes, shatter light bulbs and bottles. Anything made of glass he can splinter by simply raising his voice.

At first he uses the phenomenal gift only in self-defense. When someone tries to take away his drum, Oskar punishes him with a garbage can full of broken glass. Symbolically, Oskar's piercing scream is not only a form of protest but a criticism of society. Although in the beginning he screams only when his individuality is threatened, in later life he admits to employing his talent in pointless playfulness. He destroys solely for the joy of destruction.

Point Of View: In this chapter Grass establishes the point of view that will characterize the novel. He looks at people from below, from the bottom up rather from above down, which, of course, is not the most flattering view. Since Oskar possesses an adult's intelligence, he sees people from two perspectives. Looking at people as an adult he sees them with clear-sightedness and perspicuity, but at the same time with an adult's errors in analysis and perception. But as a clear-eyed child, he can look behind the false facade of adults and analyze their motivations.

Satire: Oskar does not have the satirist's sense of outrage, as the belief that things could be put right. He says here and elsewhere that human progress is impossible. Because, as he sees it, the world is a pointless charade without meaning or unifying principle. Not only does everything that happens defeat rational explanation but it is beyond our control. Consequently, Oskar, seeing the futility in moralizing or making value judgments, is content merely to describe what he sees and leave judgment up to the reader.

Historical Analogies: Oskar never tires of making analogies. He continually associates parallels of history with his own experience. In this chapter he sees a relationship between his first visit to Doctor Hollatz and the stock market crash in 1929. For instance, the scene at the doctor's office is an extremely elaborate pun on the word "crash," for it is there that Oskar first unleashes his glass-shattering scream and sends hundreds of alcohol bottles containing frogs, mice, and embryos "crashing" to the floor.

Characterization: Oskar's fourth birthday party is a satirical episode that characterizes the proletarian milieu. After he has screamed down all four light bulbs and plunged the apartment into darkness, the three adult couples pair off for an intoxicated orgy which is described with appropriate grotesqueness.

Grandmother Koljaiczek restores order by proposing a game of Skat. Nevertheless, the orgy continues under the card table which provides Oskar an opportunity to make certain deductions about Jan Bronski's character. With his stockinged foot, Jan probes about between Agnes' thighs, who in response moves her chair closer to the table. But although Jan is victorious beneath the table, he loses one game after another on the top. Agnes, on the other hand, while giving ground below, plays a brilliant game above.

Social **Satire**: Grass satirizes the medical profession by his treatment of the plodding, pedantic, unimaginative physician Doctor Hollatz. Although the doctor, more interested in his social position than in his profession, is unable to determine an organic cause for Oskar's inability to grow, he assures Agnes that it is due to the fall down the cellar steps. When Oskar shatters Hollatz' collection of toads and salamanders, the doctor capitalizes on this by writing a longwinded, pseudo-scientific article about it, not for the sake of disseminating knowledge but to promote his chances for a professorship.

CHAPTER SIX: THE SCHEDULE

Title: The title of this chapter refers to the schedule of learning Oskar is expected to memorize during his first and last day at school.

Theme: The schedule represents society's first organized attempt to regiment the minds of its citizens. Oskar, however, knows that true individuality will not be tolerated in modern industrialized society. Production, consumption, leisure, and all other activities must be carried out in a form ultimately beneficial to the group. Thus Oskar concludes that if he is to maintain his individuality and develop according to his own plan, he must stay out of school at all costs. This struggle between Oskar and society is symbolically advanced by his retaliation toward Miss Spollenhauer, his teacher, when she tries to take his drum away. To protect his drum - his individuality - Oskar defies her by shattering the windows and her eyeglasses. The warm spring air - freedom - rushes in and Spollenhauer, now unable to see, is forced to retreat.

Characterization: Here, as elsewhere, characterization is carried out by means of caricature. The schoolboys are pictured as a horde of ill-mannered, noisy brats who are only too eager to relinquish their individuality to the State. Miss Spollenhauer is very nearly a caricature of a caricature. Thin, reedy, and frustrated, she is the academic martinet who believes that a good education consists in breaking the will. Grass uses her to portray adults who are will-less robots. They are human only when they forget themselves and become like children once again, as does Miss Spollenhauer who, for an instant, forgets that she is a teacher. Being human to Oskar means to be child - like curious, complex, and non- moralistic. This is the unself-conscious state of man before he has been taught the suppressions, sublimations, and rationalizations adults are forced to accept to survive in a society of false values.

CHAPTER SEVEN: RASPUTIN AND THE ALPHABET

Title: This chapter refers to the way Oskar is taught to read and to his first primer, Rasputin and his Women.

Themes: Despite his performance at school, Oskar realizes the importance of learning to read so he tries vainly for several months to persuade the neighbors to teach him. Each of the adults approached, however, is incompetent because all of them lack the ability to break out of their routine. After the fiasco at the Pestalozzi school, his parents are wallowing in self-pity and bewailing the injustice of the cross - Oskar - they must bear. Greengrocer Greff is too preoccupied with his vegetables and young boys, and trumpet player Meyn, when he is not playing, is either drunk or asleep. Since to ask for help in plain language would reveal his adult intelligence and bring with it unpleasant consequences, Oskar is forced to use other means. Finally, he offers himself as a surrogate baby to Gretchen Scheffler, the childless wife of the neighborhood baker. The basically warm, exuberant, and sexy woman, however, is hopelessly plain. Ignored by her husband, she is a frustrated woman. In return for reading lessons, Oskar permits her to dress him up in the baby clothes she has knitted for her unborn child.

Oskar's problem is a difficult one. To preserve the identity of an eternal three-year-old, he must not appear to learn too rapidly. On the other hand, if he learns too slowly, Gretchen will lose patience and discontinue the lessons. This experience particularly hurts Oskar's pride because he must pretend to be even more slow-witted than his teacher.

The Grotesque As A Literary Device: Oskar insists that he be taught from only two books, *Rasputin and His Women* and Goethe's *Elective Affinities*. The former, an account of Rasputin's life at the Czar's court complete with provocative drawings and racy stories, holds Gretchen's interest as well as Oskar's. Every fourth lesson, however, Oskar demands Goethe. These two works say a great deal about Grass' novelistic technique. Rasputinism represents the grotesque in life and in human nature. Although it is a salient feature of *The Tin Drum*, it is not used to shock or upset the reader. Rasputinism is there because it exists in human society and is an essential part of society. The serious writer cannot ignore it.

Rasputin is directly contrasted to Goethe who represents everything that is beautiful, noble, and sublime in the world. When Oskar tears out pages from both books and shuffles them together like a deck of cards to create a new volume, Grass is unveiling a description of his own novelistic technique.

Oskar's Character: Finally, Oskar's reference to the "two souls" - Goethe and Rasputin - he embodies in his own breast is one of the rare hints to his character. Oskar views himself neither as all good nor as all evil, but as a mixture of the two. Consequently, he is not only unable to make arbitrary distinctions between good and evil but also unwilling to pass judgment on the inconsistencies, foibles, and weakness of those around him.

Point Of View: Oskar, taking advantage of the fact that both Gretchen and his mother are unaware of his advanced intelligence, is able to freely observe how they respond to the tales of Rasputin. As the author shows repeatedly, adults are more likely to reveal themselves as they really are when they think they are alone. Twelve pages of Rasputin so thoroughly arouse the two women that Oskar's lesson ends amid sighs, groans, and quick little gasps. It grieves Oskar to watch the two women struggling to find a normal outlet for passions that society tries to repress.

Sutterlin Script: Oskar intensely dislikes the standard German script because he feels that it reflects the undesirable characteristics of human nature. It is angular and malignant;

therefore, it is admirably suited for recording slogans, diplomas, and death sentences.

CHAPTER EIGHT: THE STOCKTURM: LONG DISTANCE SOUND EFFECTS

Title: This chapter is named after one of the many fortified medieval towers in downtown Danzig. It is from here late in the chapter that Oskar experiments with his voice and shatters the windows of the city theater.

Theme: Grass returns to social **satire** by pointing out Oskar's isolation from society. For instance, in the scene where Oskar watches some children concoct a foul soup, he thinks the recipe for this witch's brew could very well have been taken from a volume of witchcraft. The brew is first spit into three times, then, from the earth, brick dust is added. Next something living, the toads, are thrown in. Finally, needing something belonging to the cooks, their excrement is stirred in. As it develops, the soup is in reality nothing more than a reflection of the children's inner characters. They are foul, corrupt, and disgusting. Suddenly aware they are being watched, and fearing that Oskar will tell their parents, the band of urchins decides to punish him by forcing him to drink some of the soup. This **episode**, reflecting his repugnance to the repulsive soup, accurately defines Oskar's relationship to the world.

Symbolism: Shortly afterward, Oskar climbs the Stockturm and utilizes the gift of his voice to indiscriminately break windows in distant parts of the city. Concentrating his efforts on the City Theater, he reduces the front row to shards. This act can be interpreted as not only a curse uttered over the city but a prophecy of the almost total destruction that Danzig would suffer during the war.

Characterization: Oskar's mother, who is by now meeting Jan Bronski once a week in a hotel for an afternoon of lovemaking, is still regarded by both partners as basically right. But even though they are innocent, they are nevertheless sowing the seeds of their own destruction. Oskar seems to foretell future trouble when he describes their relationship as "the appetite that bites its own tail."

CHAPTER NINE: THE ROSTRUM

Title: Chapter nine, referring to the location where the Nazis hold their rallies, develops the symbol of regimentation and madness.

Bebra: On an outing to the circus, Oskar meets the fifty-three-year-old midget Bebra, a kind of miniature, omniscient Magus archetype who becomes Oskar's spiritual leader. Bebra predicts that chaotic times are ahead and that if the little people are to survive they must make it their business to be on or under the Rostrum, never in front of it. Bebra's warning refers to the policy later established by the Nazis to exterminate everyone who did not conform to certain biological standards.

Theme And Satire: Here the author satirizes the Nazi propaganda machine and its juvenile appeal. He shows that the appeal the Nazis had for their devotees was based on a fantasy which had little to do with reality. People attended the great rallies not from inner conviction but because of the typical German propensity for wanting to spend time in a worthwhile way. People simply wanted to be present when history was being made.

Characterization: Taking Bebra's suggestion seriously, Oskar attends a rally at the Maiwiese. His attention is immediately drawn toward the orator Lobsack because he is not only highly articulate but because he has a humpback. Oskar notices that Lobsack's wit and intelligence reside in his hump. He bases his political theories on his deformity and uses it to create convincing parallels such as before the Communists would be allowed to take over, he would lose his hump. In short, Lobsack regards his hump in much the same way as Oskar regards his drum. It is the organizing principle of his individuality.

Lobsack's hump also symbolizes the warped philosophy of the Nazi Party. Oskar admires the way he influences listeners and leads them to agree with the most idiotic ideas.

Satire And Symbolism: Oskar looks at the Nazi Party from the same viewpoint that he observes life, from the bottom up. Oskar's impression of the Party is formed not by listening to Lobsack but by scrutinizing the rostrum itself. The symmetrical construction of the platform displeases him immensely. It is, he thinks, much too rationally constructed and denies any opportunity for emotion. He is determined to find out the true nature of this political movement so he can understand the reasons for his dislike. It is noteworthy that Oskar forms his opinion of the party by examining what the party has actually constructed. Seen from the front, the rostrum is beautifully symmetrical and handsomely fetched out with decorations and flashy uniforms. When seen from behind and below, however it is ugly, cramped, dark, and hastily knocked together. Continuing his investigation, Oskar crawls beneath the rostrum to gather further impressions free of distractions.

With the help of his drum Oskar brings the inner nature of the Party to the surface for all to see. First, he drums the rhythm of the "Blue Danube Waltz." As the musicians above his head become confused, one by one they change from the martial music to the waltz. Then when Oskar switches to the catchy jazz-tune "Jimmy the Tiger," the crowd responds to the new rhythm by grabbing a partner and beginning to dance. When the rally ends in total chaos, the true nature of both the German people and the Nazi Party is revealed. Grass seems to be implying that among the reasons for the Nazi success was their ability to impose symmetry on the basically romantic German nature.

Characterization: The real performer in this **episode** is Lobsack. Just as the beautiful and symmetrical exterior of the rostrum belied its rotten inner core, Lobsack's reaction to Oskar's rendition of "Jimmy the Tiger" betrays his twisted and decayed inner nature. Unwilling or unable to find a suitable partner, he dances a grotesque, perverse, and savage jig. His jackboots pound the earth in vicious wrath as if snuffing out some unseen foe.

This unhallowed jig is actually a prediction of the way the German Army will grind Europe under its heel.

CHAPTER TEN: SHOPWINDOWS

Title: Although we are promised a story about shop-windows, most of the chapter deals with unrelated matters. The shopwindows are used merely to signify temptation.

Social Criticism: In a switch back to the present, Oskar viciously attacks the self-important and impotent intellectuals who refused to combat the Nazis when they were still weak. Now that the war is over, they proclaim hypocritically that although they did not resist the Party physically, they did so intellectually.

After the war they quickly invented such **cliches** as "psychic emigration" and "inward resistance" to prove they had not been taken in by the propaganda.

Leitmotif: Again, Grandmother Koljaiczek's four earth-colored skirts appear in this chapter as the symbol of refuge, security, and happiness.

Theme And Characterization: Oskar's investigations into human nature are carried out without pre-conceived notions of the results. Hiding in darkened doorways on snowy evenings, he leads window-shoppers into temptation. When a victim stops to gaze at some expensive article, Oskar "sings" a small hole next to the coveted object. Although most people take something, the effect of stealing on the conscience is remarkably similar. With few exceptions they are overcome with guilt and remorse and, after spending a sleepless night, turn themselves in to the police. This experience, however, does not restore Oskar's confidence in human nature nor does it provide him with proof that man at bottom is honest. Man is not only basically dishonest; he is also a fearful creature unable even for an instant to cross the line of acceptable morality without feelings of guilt. Church and State have so successfully programmed human beings that they are unwilling to take on themselves the responsibility of a free choice, or abide by their decisions if they do make a choice.

Oskar believes that his actions have helped people to know themselves and that the means justifies the method he has employed to open their eyes. Self-knowledge, for instance, turns the prosecuting attorney, renowned for his cruel sentences, into a compassionate and understanding jurist. Thus by showing Oskar as a composite of both good and evil, the author illuminates the polaric nature of evil. Evil in itself is a mixture of kindness and cruelty, of good will and ill will.

Biblical Language: Grass frequently uses Biblical language to good effect. For instance, after Jan Bronski removes the necklace from the shopwindow, he remains staring at the hole too long. Oskar writes: "O Father, Son, and Holy Spirit. It was high time the spirit moved, or it would be all up with Jan the father. Oskar the son unbuttoned his coat..."

CHAPTER ELEVEN: NO WONDER

Title: This chapter, entitled Kein Wunder in German, loses its ambiguous meaning in translation, for Wunder means both "wonder" and "miracle." In this chapter, Oskar asks for a miracle, and it is "no wonder" that there is "no miracle."

Theme: This chapter reveals Grass' negative attitude to organized religion, especially the Catholic Church. To be sure, the author's approach is entirely free of value judgments, indignation, and anger. Nevertheless, he succeeds in showing religion to be an absurdity.

He employs several techniques to accomplish this. The first is to bring out the contradictory nature of the sacrament of confession.

For instance, when Oskar's mother suddenly gets religious, she senses that her adulterous affair with Jan Bronski is wrong in the eyes of the Church. Although she goes once a week to confess her sins, she continues to meet Jan in the hotel room on Thursdays. She arranges matters, however, so that she can make a confession soon after her love tryst, thereby enjoying a state of grace for the next six days. Anna, however, is less criticized than the Church for propagating this hypocritical travesty by giving Agnes absolution without ordering her to discontinue the affair.

Not only are the priests portrayed as hypocritical but the Church and its doctrines are partially responsible for Agnes' death.

The reader is not supposed to take Agnes' conversion seriously. For instance, she leafs through the confessional as if it were a shopping catalog and expects the sacraments to give her a lift like a cup of coffee and a cigarette: a sort of spiritual pause that refreshes.

Ominously foretelling her doom, Oskar describes the strips of sticky flypaper hanging above her head in the store that spells death for the unwary.

Technical Devices: By ridiculing the Church through parallelism, Oskar finds lines from the Mass lodged in his brain like catchy tunes that refuse to leave. Thus he finds himself singing the praises of the Virgin in the toilet. Then the romanticized image of "Sweet Jesus" is attacked through comparison. Jesus is portrayed by the church sculptor as a well-proportioned, smooth-skinned athlete setting the world's record in the famous event known as The Stations of the Cross. One particularly obnoxious statue of Jesus shows him as a Prussian nobleman displaying his bleeding heart and stigmata like medals awarded by Kaiser Wilhelm. This disturbs Oskar, for the resemblance between this figure and Jan Bronski is particularly striking and upsetting.

Finally, the author uses syntactical devices to rob religion of dignity, as when Agnes walks to confession across "catholic flagstones," the baby Jesus sits upon the Virgin's "thigh," and Oskar pinches Jesus' "little watering can." Taking advantage of whatever religious exposure the reader may have had, Grass disturbs even those readers of little faith since no one really thinks of the Virgin Mary as having "thighs" and Jesus having a "little watering can" like other men.

Oskar As Christ Figure: Chapter Eleven contains the first indications that Grass intends to develop Oskar as a modern Christ figure. The similarity Oskar notices between Jesus and Jan Bronski (whom Oskar regards as his true father) and his inability to shatter the stained glass windows both suggest an underlying religious **theme**. Even more significant is Oskar's identification with the infant Jesus whom he approaches as an equal rather than as a supplicant.

When Oskar, seeking a private miracle, notices that the statue's hands are strangely empty, he places the drum in Jesus' lap, puts the sticks in His hands, and bids Him drum. We must remind ourselves that Oskar has the intelligence of an adult. Consequently, his actions cannot be attributed to the innocent behavior of children. Even though Jesus performs no miracle, Oskar retains a vestige of faith when his voice proves impotent against the stained glass.

CHAPTER TWELVE: GOOD FRIDAY FARE

Title: The name of this chapter refers to the eel soup which Matzerath prepares following a family excursion to the beach on Good Friday.

Theme And Characterization: In this and the following chapter, Oskar investigates the nature of his mother's guilt and the self-punishment that lead to her death. A premonition of future events is made when the street car stops at the siding next to the abandoned cemetery and Agnes remembers that she would like to be buried there if the place were still in use.

As the outing begins, Agnes is in good spirits, happy in her three roles as vivacious and sexy mistress of the handsome

Jan Bronski, competent housewife, and successful retailer. When the small group reaches the end of the breakwater and watches the loathsome way the longshoreman fishes for eels, Agnes reacts in a remarkable manner. Vomiting and retching profusely, she almost faints from nausea. But she refuses to turn away from the sickening spectacle. On their return home, Matzerath prepares their dinner from the eels that he had bought from the longshoreman. Again, Agnes's overreaction to the eel soup and the violent argument she provokes are a prelude to Chapter Thirteen.

Historical Analogy: Again, Grass projects family events onto a historical background. By the year 1937 the Nazis had completely consolidated their power in the domestic sphere. Communists and other political rivals had either emigrated or had been hunted down and sent off to extermination camps. The aristocracy and powerful industrial magnates, such as the Krupps and Thyssens, had been coerced into cooperating with the Party. The Nazis had just embarked on the foreign policy that led to the gradual disintegration of the social order and to World War II.

The Clothes Closet: Oscar occasionally needs a place where he can put his impressions into perspective. Deprived of Grandmother Koljaiczek's skirts, he finds a substitute sanctuary in the clothes closet; there he can enjoy the feeling of security and visualize a world in which all polarities are reconciled.

CHAPTER THIRTEEN: TAPERED AT THE FOOT END

Title: The title of this chapter describes the shape of a coffin and announces his mother's funeral.

Theme: Following the **episode** on Good Friday, Oskar's mother develops a perverse hunger for fish, devouring in the course of a day enormous quantities of eel, sardines, and cod. In this way she slowly and knowingly poisons herself. But why suicide? The text suggests several answers, each of which contains some truth. Matzerath believes that she is pregnant and is merely indulging a whim. He also suspects that she may not be quite sure who the father is. Anna Koljaiczek, however, claims that Matzerath and Oskar's drumming are responsible. Oskar thinks that his mother has been unconsciously looking for a way out of the love triangle that would leave Matzerath with the guilt and Jan with the feeling that she had sacrificed herself for him and his career. Yet Oskar and the omniscient drum are only partially correct.

By carefully examining the text, we are able to conclude that her illness is the culmination of a malady of the soul that has been festering for several years. Agnes is a simple peasant girl brought up in a social tradition with its strict code of what is permitted and what is not. She is unable to indefinitely live the dual role of housewife and mistress without suffering inner deterioration. Although she tries to suppress her guilt feelings, she merely succeeds in sublimating them. Her taste for sweet and viscous pastries, mocha, and fattening desserts is the first sign. When sweets no longer suffice, she turns to religion as a way to expiate her guilt. But the mechanical recitation of some piece of ancient mummery merely results in making her more aware of the predicament. Thus Agnes is receptive to any stimulus, such as the scene on the breakwater, that can portray her existence in true perspective. From Oskar's description of the scene, the progression of her reactions from astonishment to nausea to regurgitation indicates that she experiences inwardly what her senses perceive outwardly. It is nothing less than a pictorial presentation of herself. Like the horse's head, she is being devoured from within by guilt.

CHAPTER FOURTEEN: HERBERT TRUCZINSKI'S BACK

Title: The title of this chapter refers to the scars Herbert Truczinski has received in knife fights.

Theme And Historical Analogy: Herbert's scarred back serves as Oskar's means for conducting an investigation into the effect of political unrest on the private citizen. While Herbert has his lunch, Oskar touches the scars on his naked back and listens to the story connected with each. The waterfront beer joint where Herbert works as a waiter is a kind of international crossroads where sailors and longshoremen of all political ideologies and religious convictions congregate on their way to distant ports. Inevitably, political discussions ensue which frequently degenerate into brawls and knife fights. It is Herbert's self-appointed duty to break up the fights and bounce the combatants out the front door, a task he is physically well equipped to do. Nevertheless, the brawlers often turn their rage upon Herbert. The **theme** of the political discussion is then translated into engravings on Herbert's back. Symbolically, Herbert represents Danzig which always suffers indirectly when the big powers squabble.

The detailed description of each scar must not be regarded as an exercise in storytelling. In fact, Herbert's back portrays the historical events immediately preceding World War II. Herbert receives his first scar when he becomes involved in traditional East European prejudices. When a Pole insults a Ukrainian by calling him a Russian, Herbert intervenes. But, turning on him, both refer to him as a Nazi. When Herbert defends his political beliefs, the Pole stabs Herbert in the back.

The second scar reflects German diplomatic quarrels. When the British Prime Minister Chamberlain is made the butt of a joke, to the irritation of a Scottish seaman, Herbert gets it in the back. Again, Herbert becomes symbolically involved in European religious quarrels when he receives a wound in a fight in front of the Seaman's Church.

Herbert's primary motivation in interfering in other people's arguments is to establish peace. If we regard him as a representative of the European common man, then we may say that the general attitude is a preference for peace. Grass, however, suggests that in the modern age the individual cannot avoid involvement in politics nor the responsibility for such involvement. Herbert quits his job, overcome by remorse and guilt, because he accidentally kills a Latvian sea captain. That such transgressions must somehow be punished, regardless of the circumstances, is illustrated in the next chapter.

Oskar's Satanism: Oskar continues to provide more evidence so that a fuller understanding of his character can be achieved. The midget Bebra, Oskar's master and teacher, reappears in Danzig with a touring circus and his girlfriend, Roswitha Raguna, both of whom possess a remarkable power. They can look inside a person and discern that individual's inmost nature. When Roswitha looks into Oskar's soul, she recoils in terror at what she sees there. Upset by her terror, Bebra explains that it is the diabolical element in Oskar's genius that has frightened her. This is not news to Oskar for it will be recalled that he often converses with a part of himself whom he calls "Satan." He regards it as particularly provident, however, that "Satan" was not driven out during the baptismal ceremony. Oskar's diabolical element will become increasingly evident as he becomes indirectly responsible for the death of those closest to him, and finally, directly responsible for Matzerath's death.

Oskar's Guilt: In this chapter Oskar admits to feelings of guilt and a certain responsibility for his mother's death. He feels that his decision to stop growing at age three was one of the factors contributing to her premature death.

CHAPTER FIFTEEN: NIOBE

Title: In classical mythology, Niobe was daughter of Tantalus and wife of Amphion, the king of Thebes. Proud of her many beautiful children, she felt herself superior to the goddess Leto who had only two. Enraged, Leto's two children, Apollo and Artemis, killed all but two of Niobe's children before her eyes. Thereupon, Zeus changed Niobe into a stone. In this form she wept over her dead children. In this chapter the name Niobe has been given to the figurehead of a Dutch maiden who in 1417 was burned for posing in the nude. Local superstition holds that the dead girl's spirit inhabits the figurehead and wreaks vengeance on the living.

Theme: Herbert has taken a new job as guard in the Maritime Museum where the figurehead Niobe is also kept. Grass draws a close parallel between this figurehead and the history of Danzig. Long after she was placed in the museum, mysterious deaths have been associated with her, twelve in the last fourteen years. After establishing Niobe as a historical symbol, Grass returns to the **theme** of the individual's relationship to history. In the first days, Oskar and Herbert purposely ignore the figure. Growing weary of this, they decide to insult her. Accordingly, Oskar beats her with his drumsticks while Herbert drives nails into her. Finally, they don historical costumes and act out historical events before Niobe's amber eyes. In a way she is also made to come alive and to take part. The author describes Niobe's awakening by explaining the manner in which the afternoon sun illuminates her eyes. Then the convex lens catches the sunshine and "ignites" the model ships in the gallery. Thus, by inciting Niobe and setting a fire, Oskar and Herbert become symbolically involved in politics and history.

The **episode** of Herbert's impalement and grotesque death on the figurehead is Grass' way of portraying how history gradually involves even the apolitical and that such involvement cannot be avoided. In Grass' philosophy of history and politics, all who participate, willingly or unwillingly, are equally guilty and must suffer the consequences.

CHAPTER SIXTEEN: FAITH, HOPE, LOVE

Title: A night of smashing, plundering, and murder emphasizes the incongruity of her title.

Theme And Analysis: At the end of the previous chapter, Oskar promises Bruno that he will make less noise with his drum. Yet after the frenzied dictation of Chapter Sixteen, his drum is reduced to scrap.

This chapter begins with the traditional fairy-tale "once upon a time" which in varying forms is repeated over two dozen times within the space of a few pages. Grass is emphasizing the infantile nature of what is to follow.

On the night of November 9, 1938, on direct orders from Goebbels, the SA attacked Jewish shops and synagogues all over Europe, a "spontaneous" demonstration against international Jewry. Troopers wreck Sigismund Markus' toyshop and would have murdered the old man himself had he not first taken poison. The infantile nature of that evening, and by implication the Nazi movement, is symbolized by the events in the toyshop. The troopers cut open dolls, smash toys, and deport themselves like any child who finds himself alone in a toyshop. Their ultimate stupidity is revealed in writing "Jew Sow" on the shop window before breaking it. But it is really in the Sutterlin script in which the epithet is written that Oskar sees the malignant nature of the movement.

And again, the paradoxical nature of National Socialism is brought out by Meyn's actions when he returns home from Herbert's funeral. In a fit of grief, he kills his four pet tom cats with a poker and is subsequently expelled from the SA for cruelty to animals.

Characterization: Before recounting the events of that night, Oskar first turns each **protagonist** into a fairy tale figure by beginning each **episode** with "once upon a time." The story and comments are then interrupted by further comments in which the characters appear again in the present. Finally, each account is closed by another "once upon a time." The chapter itself ends with the closing of the traditional German fairy tale "And if they aren't dead, they're still alive." Grass implies hereby that the **protagonists** are entirely independent of each other and each has his own individual story. At the conclusion, however, they are all brought together for one fatal moment, much as in Thornton Wilder's The Bridge at San Luis Rey.

The first "once upon a time" deals with Meyn who as a civilian was constantly drunk. Even so, he had the ability to play the trumpet too beautifully for words. After lending his talent to the SA and renouncing alcohol, he still retained his musical ability but he lost his feeling for music. Instead he plays marches. Meyn has sought to bring order into his life by giving up alcohol and by joining an organization that is proud of its order and symmetry. He pays a terrible price, however, for he has lost his soul. Schugger Leo, a harmless eccentric who hangs about graveyards, perceives this transformation. When Meyn discovers that his inner life is still an abyss, he turns upon his cats regarding them as the symbol of his own inner bestiality. It is noteworthy that even after he has cleaned up after the deed, the pungent odor of tomcats, for which his room is famous, is as strong as ever, thus indicating the failure of his efforts.

Significantly, one of the cats is named Bismarck. This possibly refers to Kaiser Wilhelm II's dismissal of Bismarck which led to a change in foreign policy and to World War I.

THE TIN DRUM

BOOK TWO

....

CHAPTER ONE: SCRAP METAL

Title: The title both refers to Oskar's drum which in the previous chapter received a furious beating and is an **allusion** to the approaching war which will have an insatiable appetite for scrap.

Characterization: Changing once again to the present, Oskar uses this chapter to connect Book I to Book II. He briefly summarizes the effect of his past experiences on his spirit and sets the stage for what is to follow. We discover almost parenthetically that he is the father of a teenage son. This information is presented so casually that the reader recognizes how indifferent Oskar is to this fact. Oskar is much more interested in the new drum that Maria brings. The ritual surrounding its unwrapping reveals that Oscar attaches almost religious significance to it. It is first unwrapped by loosening the strings and permitting the wrapping paper to unfold of its own accord. The washing it receives in the basin resembles a baptism. In fact, Oskar immediately uses the drum to transport himself back to a time when he could crawl under Grandmother Koljaiczek's skirts, a place we know he regards as the primary source of being.

The reader also gains insight into Oskar's personal feelings toward the instrument. Returning once again to the past, Oskar explains that he suffers from a neurotic fear of being left without a supply of drums. So acute is this fear that since 1949 (he is writing in 1954), he stores his battered-up drums in the potato cellar. The cause of this fear can be directly related to the events immediately preceding World War II.

Theme And Historical Events: Since the death of his mother and Sigismund Markus, Oskar has been deprived of his source of drums. On August 31, 1939, he waits for Jan Bronski to take him to the janitor Kobyella at the Polish Post Office. The following day, September 1, the Waffer SS laid siege to the building (an actual historical event) and the German Armies invaded Poland. Oskar's difficulties in securing a new drum are played out against this backdrop.

CHAPTER TWO: POLISH POST OFFICE

Title: The title refers to the siege and fall of the Polish Post Office on September 1, 1939.

Theme: In an elaborate scenario, Oskar's drumming and the war games are correlated. Once inside the building, Oskar notices with his adult intelligence that the preparations under way for the battle resemble a game. The defenders laugh and shout, encourage one another, and declare themselves ready to die for their country. Oskar too attempts to take part in the game, marching up and down the corridor like a little general inspecting his troops. But he also sees that the game is pointless and that the defenders are doomed.

Oskar draws an analogy between the battle for the Polish Post Office and Poland. To heighten the effect, he describes the festive atmosphere in Danzig on the day before the attack. While one group of people amuse themselves at the beach, drink tea, and eat ice cream, another group is furiously fortifying the building.

The only person who does not fit into this scene is Jan Bronski. He is the archetypal civilian who is so impractical that he cannot sharpen a pencil properly. Ironically, his civilian clothes are his undoing. When he approaches the cordon of soldiers blocking the entrance to the post office, Jan thinks that he and Oskar will be turned back. He will then be able to justify his absence from the defense of the building while playing the hero. Instead he is permitted to pass because of his fine clothes. The soldiers never suspect that the nattily dressed gentleman with a three-year-old child at his side could also be a Polish partisan. Inside the building Jan discovers that he is distrusted by his colleagues who suspect him of shirking his duty to Poland.

Oskar follows the course of the battle by focusing his attention on the protagonist's legs. Kobyella, for instance, uses his wooden leg to inspire courage in Jan who is afraid to fight. In an effort to make himself unfit for combat, Jan exposes his leg to rifle fire. The running, shuffling, and dragging of legs tell Oskar how the battle is progressing.

Characterization: Grass illuminates character by showing the individual's reaction to war. For instance, Kobyella is transformed from a janitor into a courageous killer. During the battle he assumes the role of leader over those who are his superiors in civilian life. As a soldier, he physically experiences war and consequently suffers a physical wound. By contrast, Jan Bronski experiences combat in a spiritual way. Every exploding artillery shell and each rifle shot, regardless of its intended victim, wounds Jan's heart. He lies on the floor, shrieks, screams, and weeps at each explosion. This should not be regarded as cowardice, for he is not afraid of being wounded. In fact, he exposes his leg to rifle fire, thereby signifying his willingness to sacrifice the one thing which had always made him victorious, his leg.

CHAPTER THREE: THE CARD HOUSE

Title: The third chapter takes its name from the house of cards Jan builds before the soldiers enter the room.

Theme And Characterization: In this chapter, the battle for the Polish Post Office is described from a different angle. Kobyella is mortally wounded and Jan's mind is unhinged by the exploding shells. Both men are placed with the other dead, rather appropriately, in the dead-letter office. In some of his best prose, Grass describes the pathetic scene that takes place in that room. With Oskar, Jan and Kobyella play Skat until the post office is captured. For once Oskar drops all pretenses, acts like an adult, plays Skat skillfully, and converses articulately. In the card game the roles are once again reversed. While during the battle Jan was bullied by Kobyella and forced to become the subservient and unwilling soldier, he now assumes the dominant role and forces Kobyella to play cards. The janitor is tied upright to a mail basket and is dealt a hand. Mortally wounded, he is understandably uninterested in the game. To attract his attention he is punched, abused, shouted at, and is not permitted the Hollywood death he longs for. During the game Oskar experiences a remarkable sense of responsibility toward Jan that he has never felt before. He realizes that it is only the card game which protects his presumptive father from the terror of the shells and preserves his sanity. For the first time in his life Oskar sacrifices his own preferences to accommodate someone else. With ironic understatement, Oskar is quick to point out the significance of his sacrifice since he has a splitting headache and would rather take a nap.

The perpetual loser Bronski is dealt his first and last Grand Slam. But he is not permitted the satisfaction of playing the winning hand because Kobyella dies. His death signifies not only the end of the card game but also the end of Poland. Finally, Jan builds an elaborate, three-tiered house from the cards, surmounted by the King and Queen of Hearts symbolizing Jan and Agnes. Significantly, his love for Agnes and indeed, his entire life, is blown apart by the currents set up by the German soldiers opening the door with their shouts of 'raus! Oskar's disdain for German obtuseness and lack of refinement is apparent from his description of the final scene. Preferring concrete to architectural finesse, the soldiers fail to see the card house. They then make fools of themselves shouting 'raus to lifeless bodies.

Oskar's Guilt: Partial responsibility for his mother's death is now coupled with the death of Jan Bronski. Even though Oskar loves his father, he is unwilling to come to his aid. While the soldiers are clearing out the dead-letter office, Oskar inveigles himself into the soldier's compassion by sniveling and pointing an accusing finger at Jan. The quick-witted soldiers immediately conclude that the three-year-old child was being used as a human shield in typically ruthless Polish fashion. As the prisoners are being herded into the courtyard for the benefit of the German newsreels, Oskar remembers that as a child he cannot be held responsible for his actions. Completely abandoning his father, he throws a fit and is hustled off to the hospital. As Oskar is driven from the scene, Jan waves good-bye still holding the Queen of Hearts, Oskar's symbolic leave-taking from both parents. Oskar so values his secret identity that he refuses to lift his disguise at any price.

CHAPTER FOUR: HE LIES IN SASPE

Title: Chapter Four takes its title from the abandoned cemetery where Jan Bronski is buried following his execution.

Theme And Characterization: Oskar enlarges upon themes introduced in the last chapter. Although he suffers immensely from his betrayal of Jan, his pride and thirst for freedom will not permit him to make an effort to save his father from death. Relatives visit him in the hospital and attempt to communicate the gravity of the situation, but Oskar refuses to abandon his imitation of the three-year-old. The presence of Jan's relatives is so painful that he pretends convulsions so that he will be forbidden visitors. Consequently, the man whom he regards as his true father is executed for irregular military activities.

The manner in which the family learns of Jan's execution betrays Grass' cynicism. Hedwig receives a letter from the Inspector of Courts-Martial. The communication announces Jan's death, but does not reveal the whereabouts of the grave. Oskar imagines that the Germans think this to be a highly considerate act, for in this way they spare the family the financial burden of a funeral.

Oskar learns the location of Bronski's grave from Leo Schugger, the man from whom no funeral can be kept secret.

Although no words pass between them, the information is transmitted through symbols of the cartridge case and the Skat card, the seven of spades. We remember that the seven of spades was the card that Jan lost in the dead-letter office and that was found by Oskar. In the occult art of telling fortunes by cards, the seven of spades, along with the nine and the ace, signifies death. It is significant that Oskar hands him this card in the post office, thus symbolizing his role in Jan's death. The cartridge case is described as "tapered at the front end." This description gives reverse meaning to a previous chapter entitled "Tapered at the Foot End." Carrying Oskar's object **metaphor** a step further, we arrive at the cynical dictum: Objects tapered at the front end lead to objects tapered at the foot end. For the second time in his life Oskar drops his secret identity, this time just long enough to tell his Grandmother where Jan is buried.

Narration Of Historical Events: Oscar deals with the problem of narrating historical events in a masterful way. The problem as he saw it was to give an accurate portrayal of the defeat of Poland without resorting to traditional means of description. Since the war, authors and historians, who attempted to convey the pointless bloodbath of those three weeks, achieved this either by letting dry statistics speak for themselves or by narrating one individual's experiences. The traditional form of description, however, has become too familiar and threadbare to be effective. Germans, and especially Poles, vividly remember the appalling spectacle of Polish cavalry attacking the German Panzers. Grass solves the problem by creating the figure of Pan Kichot, the Polish Don Quixote, who sees the tanks as windmills. Grass conveys the slaughter by **metaphor**: "So rode the squadrons out against the grey steel foe, adding another dash of red to the sunset glow." The macabre poetical translation of the scene is a very effective device to adequately reflect recent history.

Grass' Philosophy Of History: Grass sometimes views history as a force that is moving toward a specific future goal. There is occasional evidence that history has a grand plan it seeks to fulfill although it is ignorant of the means to attain it. Nevertheless, overall progress is discernible. At other times it appears as if history is a mindless, unfeeling juggernaut with no Golden Age in view, a history that repeats itself and regresses as often as it progresses. The role assigned to a human being in either case is that of pawn. The individual has little influence on the course of events and is used by history unscrupulously. Even such an imposing figure as Adolf Hitler is seen as an unimportant cog obediently carrying out the task assigned to him. Grass relegates Hitler's unimportance by putting his name at the end of a long and involved participial phrase. Despite Ralph Mannheim's really good translation of the novel, this syntactical device simply cannot be rendered in English.

CHAPTER FIVE: MARIA

Title: This chapter introduces Herbert Truczinski's sister. Recalling the Biblical Mary, she symbolizes innocence and the end of Oskar's virginity.

Characterization: Maria is one of Grass' more successful women figures. He uses her to reflect World War II and, later, recent German history. As a representative of the post-war German, it is perhaps significant that her character is nondescript.

Theme: In this chapter, the tin drum is accorded yet another function: expiating guilt. Oskar regards the new drum which he rescued at the Polish Post Office as a witness to his betrayal of Jan. No matter how he plays, its only **refrain** is betrayal.

The only way out of the dilemma is to destroy the drum, not by discarding it, but by reducing it to scrap. In destroying the drum, he believes he can end his guilt feelings. So beginning in October, he drums furiously until at the beginning of December the drum is destroyed and his guilt along with it.

In this way the drum assumes religious significance and resembles the recitation of penances. According to Catholic dogma if, following the confession of sin, the penitent executes the prescribed penances in the proper way, guilt will be expiated. Therefore, by beating his drum, Oskar "confesses" his transgressions while destroying his guilt.

Oskar expects but does not receive a new drum at Christmas simply because everyone is weary of the noise. The implications for Oskar, however, are far-reaching. He is deprived of his means of communication with the outside world and with himself. It may be asked why he does not resort to the simple stratagem of taking the necessary money from the cash box and buying his own drum: Again religious considerations prevent him from doing so. As a receptacle for guilt, the drum must be innocent. To acquire a drum through dishonest means would soil it and deprive it of its function.

Love: Maria is Oskar's first love. Despite her non-descript mental and physical attributes, Oskar, somewhat unwillingly, discovers a growing passion for her. Significantly, it is his drum that first makes him aware of his feelings. Not only does Oskar communicate with the outside world through his drum, it is a means of looking within himself. Closely connected to these feelings is the awakening sexual urge. These unfamiliar sensations are described through:

Color Symbolism: In the evenings Maria undresses Oskar, washes him and puts him to bed. Since he is a fully developed male in most respects, the evening bath makes Oscar blush deeply for several minutes. As we noted earlier, Grass associates the color red with transgression, sex, and guilt. Grandfather Koljaiczek blushed whenever the word "match" or "fire" was mentioned, while Anna turned crimson when reminded of her first encounter with her husband beneath the four skirts.

Symbolism Of Odors: Oskar associates specific odors with women. His grandmother smells of rancid butter, Mrs. Kater of ammonia, and Maria, he discovers, reminds him of vanilla. The source of this scent is a mystery to Oskar, for Maria neither likes vanilla nor uses it in cooking. Oskar solves the mystery in the grotesque scene that takes place in the bathhouse. Beneath the aroma of vanilla is the smell of earth.

CHAPTER SIX: FIZZ POWDER

Title: This chapter takes its title from a fizz powder popular during the Nazi era.

Theme And Characterization: The description of the fizz powder places in perspective the personal and historical events occurring in this chapter. The powder, obtainable in grocery stores and refreshment stands, costs three pfennigs a packet. When water was added the powder seethed, boiled, and fizzed. Owing to its indeterminate flavor and its incapacity to sustain itself, the powder was bought only by people too poor to afford a more expensive refreshment. In brief, the powder is characterized as a cheap, pretentious substitute. Into this context Oskar places his adolescent love affair and the historical events of the Nazi era.

Oskar's first love is dominated by the powder which serves as a surrogate for lovemaking. Maria places the powder either in her hand or in her navel. Oskar then brings the powder to boil with his saliva. The manner in which Maria responds clearly indicates that she experiences the sensation as a sexual release.

Despite the strong sexual nature of this chapter, it is strangely unsexual in character; nor are the descriptions titillating. This may be attributed to Oskar's particular view of sex. Having observed his mother in bed with either Matzerath or Jan Bronski, the act appears to him as nothing more than a tangle of sweating, copulating bodies accompanied by sighs, groans, and strange little noises. In short, grotesque. Sex is presented in this way throughout the novel.

Oskar's lengthy discourse on his "third drumstick" is actually a character analysis executed according to the requirements of good literature. In this way a new **protagonist** is introduced. This "individual" is described as a person with its own will and personality. The frequent changes from first person to second and even third emphasize that this object functions independently of Oskar's personal will. As the novel progresses, this new character forces him to relinquish the exclusive right to determine his actions, feelings, and the course of events.

CHAPTER SEVEN: SPECIAL COMMUNIQUES

Title: During World War II, German radio broadcasts were frequently interrupted by short news bulletins. These "Special Communiques" as they were called usually announced the latest German victory.

Historical Analogy: This chapter commences like many others with a quick turn to the present. This tactic enables the writer to contrast situations that prevailed in 1940 with those in 1954. After dictating the previous chapter to his drum, Oskar, in a fit of nostalgia, sent Bruno out to buy a packet of fizz powder but Bruno finds it is no longer made although shopkeepers remember that it was once sold during the Hitler era. They thereby unwittingly put that entire period into the same context with the cheap fizz powder. Bruno is offered a Coke instead, a more "sophisticated" substitute. As the fizz powder characterizes the Nazi era, Coca-Cola is an amusing reflection on post-war Germany.

Characterization: Nevertheless, the hospital lab technician makes some powder so that Oskar can conduct his experiment. When Maria arrives on visiting day, he pours some of the powder into her palm and tries to awaken old feelings by spitting in her hand. That Maria scuttles away in terror and will not be reminded of their earlier relationship symbolizes modern Germany's refusal to be associated with its Nazi past. Grass viciously condemns those who deny their own responsibility for what happened in the Hitler era. In fact, Maria represents the modern Germany. She dresses well but discreetly, has faith in the economic miracle, and subscribes to fashion magazines.

Theme: Returning to the narration of past events, Oskar speculates upon the identity of Kurt's father. Oskar views himself as the true father because it was a week later that he discovers Matzerath and Maria on the sofa. The grotesque scene that Oskar interrupts once again displays the author's capacity to combine story-telling with characterization. First, the act of making love is deprived of any romantic considerations. The two bodies are sprawled among rumpled clothes and dirty underwear. While Maria squeals, Matzerath emulates a rooting pig. The rhythm is punctuated with pleas of "be careful." The **climax** is reached when Oskar furiously mounts the heap of sweating bodies and pounds his drum on his father's back. Matzerath, of course, is "not careful" and the scene ends in mutual recriminations.

Oskar loses his first love to Matzerath. He tries to comfort Maria and distract her attention from Matzerath's self-righteous justifications by fetching a packet of fizz powder and spitting in her hand. Oskar receives a kick in the chest for his trouble. Two months later Matzerath and Maria are married, both convinced that Matzerath is the father. Yet the true parenthood is purposely left uncertain. Oskar claims responsibility by virtue of the fact that he was the first. It will be remembered, however, that during the shouting match with Matzerath, Maria makes a parenthetical **allusion** to a "previous time," thereby implying at least the possibility that Oskar suffers from delusions of grandeur. Nevertheless, Oskar claims responsibility to the very last.

Historical **Parody**: The entire scene is also a parody of history. The obscene, inglorious fornicating on the sofa is paralleled to the "Special Communiques" proclaiming the glorious victories of the U Boats in the North Atlantic. Historical events are thus trivialized by announcing them to the accompaniment of copulation.

Social Criticism: This chapter is also a veiled criticism of the double standard that presents war as a character-building phenomenon while fornicating is regarded as a corrupting influence. Yet here as elsewhere the author does not moralize on social standards. He merely places them in a context that illuminates their contradictory nature and leaves the reader to draw his own conclusions.

CHAPTER EIGHT: HOW OSKAR TOOK HIS HELPLESSNESS TO MRS. GREFF

Title: The reader expects that Oskar goes to Lina Greff, the greengrocer's wife, to be helped. As it turns out, Oskar's "helplessness" revolves around his need for a woman.

Characterization: Oskar interrupts the forward movement of the narrative to indulge his talent for characterization.

Greengrocer Greff is an eccentric vegetarian, pederast, and nature buff. He harbors an emotional attachment to his produce and describes potatoes and cabbages with poetic hyperbole. Before the war he spent his free time as a Scout Leader, singing songs and, to say the least, worshiping the bodies of his young troopers. The fact that he enjoys swimming in the frozen Baltic during the winter and romping naked in the snow with his scouts provides the neighborhood with considerable material for gossip. Greff is generally misunderstood. His effort to build up his clientele by attaching a contraption to his potato scales that plays popular folk tunes merely results in arousing the suspicions of the Bureau of Weights and Measures. Frequent visits by these officials drive away many of his old customers.

The dinner following Kurt's baptism is the occasion for further characterization. The guests attack the food with revolting proletarian gusto. Wielding the silverware like weapons, they glut themselves on soup, goose, and chocolate pudding. The room is filled with sounds of slurping, belching, and gnawing.

Historical Analogy: Enraged by the thought that his son will bear the name Matzerath, Oskar makes several attempts to bring about a miscarriage. He first topples a ladder on which Maria is working, resulting in a painful sprain. In the background the radio announces the German paratroop attack on Crete. The most famous casualty is the world's heavyweight champion Max Schmeling who, like Maria, suffered a sprained ankle in his descent. Oskar's second futile attempt to induce a premature birth with a pair of scissors coincides with the successful conclusion of the Crete campaign.

Kurt's baptism takes place during the battle of Smolensk on the Eastern front where many units received their first baptism of fire.

The upsurge in military activity, the demands of war on the economy, and the effects of National Socialism on the common citizen are kept in the background, thematically as well as syntactically. The growing scarcity of food is quietly and ominously noted by the increase in the number of rabbits raised in the courtyard. The movement of immense numbers of troops to the Eastern front is discernible only by the fact that people now find it difficult to travel by train. The soldier Fritz Truckzinski provides the final **allusion**. Throughout the novel he has served as a kind of weathervane for German military exploits. Always present at the latest victory, he sends postcards from Paris, Norway, Belgium, Italy, and Greece. The latest card arrives from Russia.

National Socialist preoccupation with racial purity is reflected in the Bronskis. When Germany annexed portions of Poland and Czechoslovakia, all new citizens with non-German names were encouraged to adopt Germanic ones. The Bronskis mention, again parenthetically, the submission of a petition to change their name to Ehlers.

CHAPTER NINE: 165 LBS.

Title: 165 lbs. is the exact weight of Albrecht Greff, the greengrocer. The figure is his cynical comment on his "difficulties" with the Bureau of Weights and Measures.

Theme And Characterization: Oskar describes his involvement with Lina Greff and concludes with Greff's suicide. Oskar again uses historical **metaphor** to describe his activities in Lina's bed. Just as the German Army bogs down in the mud of Russia, Oskar becomes mired in the muddy terrain of Lina's body. The lovemaking is described in the now familiar grotesque way. The affair contributes nothing to Oskar's development; it serves merely to fulfill a physical need.

During the past few months, Greff has undergone a change brought about by a new Nazi policy. He no longer takes care of his business and spends his time tinkering with his noise-making contraptions and inventions. The Nazis, in order to insure that the young people would receive proper indoctrination, have outlawed all youth organizations and absorbed them into the Hitler Jugend. Consequently, Greff was forced to disband his Boy Scout troop. It appears that he lived not only with but also through the youngsters. Deprived of their rejuvenating influence, he begins to grow old and crotchety. The summons to appear in court on a morals charge precipitates his decision to commit suicide, and he decides to use the occasion to get even with the officials from the Bureau of Weights and Measures. He constructs an elaborate machine with himself as counterweight. When his body is cut down, the mechanism plays a weird symphony, culminating in the release of 165 lbs. of potatoes. The sign proclaiming "165 lbs. (less 3 oz.)" specifies both the weight of his own body and that of the potatoes. The "less 3 oz."

reminds the reader that the sign weighs three ounces and should be subtracted from the total weight of the potatoes.

CHAPTER TEN: BEBRA'S THEATER AT THE FRONT

Title: The title refers to Bebra's troupe of touring midgets which Oskar joins.

Historical Parallels: Oskar at last finds a positive way of looking at the war. He regards it as an immense geography course in which he is informed, through the "Special Communiques," of the importance of such places as the Volga, Atu, and the Philippines. Again, the author conveys the progress of the war through minor details such as the lower quality food Matzerath prepares, the conversion of certain buildings into hospitals, and the appearance of such place names as Stalingrad and El Alamein.

Theme: The midget Bebra is now a captain in the Wehrmacht attached to a propaganda company. The course of the war-effort is reflected in Bebra's importance. As Germany's military position deteriorates, the need for effective propaganda increases. Consequently, Bebra has an official car at his disposal and even a private compartment on the furlough train. With a view to enlarging his act, Bebra once again invites Oskar to join his touring troupe. This time he enlists the aid of Roswitha Raguna who has apparently changed her mind about the diabolical element in Oskar's genius. Seduced by her charms, Oskar accepts the invitation.

Characterization: Apollo And Dionysus: Making preparations for the journey, Oskar gives us another glimpse into his character. While packing he becomes involved in an argument with two parts of his personality whom he refers to as Apollo and Dionysus. The terms are appropriate for he uses them in their Nietzschean **connotation**. It will be remembered that Nietzsche sees these two deities as the personification of opposing tendencies in man. Although in opposition to each other, each stimulates the other. In a way, the two tendencies are interdependent. Briefly, the Apollonian tendency seeks to impose order upon the world by placing all separate units in an ordered and comprehensible relation to each other. Apollo, therefore, represents the voice of reason. Dionysus, on the other hand, signifies the destruction of order resulting in chaos. The Dionysiac state is one in which the boundaries between individuals are erased. Its object is to achieve a mystical union with the universe. The cosmos itself is conceived as a unity, not as a series of individual parts. As opposed to Apollo, the Dionysian element urges the individual to obey the voice of feeling. According to Nietzsche, the ideal individual tries to achieve a balance between the two.

We see these two tendencies at work in Oskar. The voice of Apollo wants him to remain in Danzig altogether, pointing out that the trip is a highly dangerous undertaking and not at all in accordance with his spiritual development. Dionysus, of course, urges him to go, reminding him how much fun it will be. Oskar even consults the two deities about what reading matter to take, Rasputin or Goethe. Dionysus identifies himself with the former while Apollo speaks for the latter. Oskar's decision to take both must not be interpreted as a compromise. It signifies his effort to maintain a balance between the two, to never permit one tendency to gain the upper hand. Thus Grass has constructed Oskar's character according to the requirements of Greek tragedy and Nietzschean doctrine.

Novel Of Education: Grass' **parody** of the *Novel of Education* properly begins at this point. One of the requirements of this literary **genre** is exposure to the theater. Oskar's experience commences in Berlin during an air raid. The optimistic principle of the *Novel of Education*, however, clashes with and is defeated by the principle of the *Theater of the Absurd*. The midgets perform a farcical routine in an air-raid cellar before hundreds of laughing soldiers while Berlin is being reduced to rubble.

CHAPTER ELEVEN: INSPECTION OF CONCRETE, OR MYSTICAL, BARBARIC, BORED

Title: The words Mystical, Barbaric, Bored that Corporal Lankes has inscribed on the concrete pillbox becomes the epithet of our century.

Theme And Characterization: Oskar becomes a favorite of the occupation troops in Paris with his popular act that has become more sophisticated in that it is now conceived along historical lines. Furthermore, he has graduated from smashing crude German beer bottles to splintering fine French glassware. Nevertheless, his wanton destruction of irreplaceable works of art is a reminder of the way the German Army behaved in occupied territory.

On a tour of the Atlantic defenses, the midgets are introduced to Corporal Lankes and Lieutenant Herzog, who expose them to the barbaric element in the twentieth century. From Lankes they learn that living puppies are put into the concrete gun-emplacements to make them impregnable. The fact that this cruel, superstitious custom popular in medieval times, should be revived by the National Socialists is entirely in character. Furthermore, this detail is but a prelude to a more frightening event. Herzog, spying several nuns collecting shells and crabs on the beach, imagines they could be English infiltrators. Even though the nuns have been a common sight for several weeks, Herzog remembers an order that civilians are not permitted on the beaches so he orders his corporal to shoot them. Lankes says the order is senseless, but Herzog insists. Lankes shrugs his shoulders and kills them. In this way war crimes are committed; indifferently, without passion or remorse by normal, average men.

The "mystical" portion of the title is mirrored in the oblique formations Lankes has idly engraved in the concrete. The representations are senseless and without substance, form, or organizing principle. Yet if one looks closely and interprets them in the light of the title the message is unmistakable: they are meaningless.

To convey the sense of boredom, Grass has appropriately chosen military duty at an isolated outpost. Lankes has spent four years waiting for an invasion which, when it does come, overruns Dora 7 in the matter of a few minutes. The problem goes much deeper, however. Lankes' dull job is merely a symbol for the way the vast majority of humans live out their lives in intellectually stifling occupations, performing tasks that are in themselves meaningless.

Theater Of The Absurd: Oskar interrupts his narrative to present the events in the form of play, using the technique of the absurd theater. Many authors regard this **genre** as the only adequate way of representing reality. So Grass, too, dispenses with the traditional approach of describing events in a rational, composed way. His language appropriately reflects the meaning of the chapter: absurd, incoherent, devoid of logic.

Language: Oskar's poem, which Kitty recites, further reflects Grass' attitude to language. The poem is a series of loosely connected images and verbal associations which optimistically look forward to the security and easy life awaiting those who survive the war.

Oskar's Guilt: Oskar is again indirectly responsible for the death of someone near him. Awaiting a truck that is to evacuate the midgets on the morning of the Normandy invasion, Roswitha asks Oskar to bring her coffee from a motorized field kitchen. When he refuses she goes herself, arriving there at the same moment a shell from a naval gun makes a direct hit. Although at this point Oskar pretends indifference and ignorance, he nevertheless holds himself responsible.

Symbolism Of Odors: Although Oskar becomes homesick in Paris, he refuses to admit it. The alert reader will note that his description of the smells of Paris betrays his longing. The city, and particularly the Metro, has the distinct aroma of rancid butter, an odor he associates with Grandmother Koljaiczek who in turn represents security, warmth, and home. Admiring the Paris skyline from atop the Eiffel tower, his thoughts automatically return to his grandmother's four potato-colored skirts. If we wished to force the symbolism, we might say that the Metro reminds Oskar of the womb, especially since the odor of rancid butter is particularly strong there.

Oskar adds a new item to the growing list of women and odors: Roswitha's scent of cinnamon, crushed cloves, and nutmeg.

Grass' Art: Oskar's performances before the troops contains an allusion to Grass' own literary style. Oskar constructs his act according to French history. Beginning with Louis XIV and continuing through the Revolution to the present day, Oskar shatters expensive glassware looted from castles. The subtle, historical significance of his performance is lost on the guffawing, uneducated, common troops. Yet those occasional connoisseurs in the audience applaud Oskar's finesse. In fact, Oskar is particularly delighted by praise from the knowledgeable and enjoys playing only to those capable of understanding his art. This accurately describes Grass' style. The beginning student often asks why an author feels he must disguise, or hide what he has to say behind symbols, metaphors, and syntactical refinements. It is precisely such devices that distinguish literature from one-dimensional works. Grass' style is much like Oskar's performance. It can be enjoyed as pure entertainment or, for those who have trained their faculties to a higher level of perception, his art can be appreciated layer by layer for its immense wealth.

CHAPTER TWELVE: THE IMITATION OF CHRIST

Title: The title suggests that Oskar's actions in this chapter will somehow resemble those of Christ. The opposite is true. Oskar as the Messiah is imitated by Christ.

Theme: This chapter marks the emergence of Oskar as a modern Christ figure. Until the end of the novel, when Oskar at age thirty decides that he must go out into the world and gather disciples, the Christ motif plays an increasingly important role.

The parallel to Christ commences the moment Oskar returns home on his son's third birthday. The whipping he receives at Kurt's hand is a reference to Christ's scourging. The question of Oskar's dual paternity arises again, calling forth further comparisons.

That Oskar considers himself superior to Christ is evident from his behavior at the church. Standing before the plaster statue depicting Christ sitting on the Virgin's thigh, he compares himself to the infant and concludes that both he and Jesus look exactly alike. Especially similar is the precocious expression around the eyes. Throughout the comparison, Oskar is the standard to which Jesus is compared rather than the other way round. With a view to humiliating his rival, Oskar climbs up and places the drum in His hands, backs away, and defies Him to play. Which he does much to Oskar's consternation. Not amateurishly, but professionally. Jesus' performance is a medley of not only Oskar's favorite melodies but also a kind of odyssey through Oskar's life, ending with a comment on his feelings about Grandmother Koljaiczek's skirts. Finally, in a reference to St. Peter, Oskar denies Jesus three times, whereupon he is appointed His successor. Oskar's reaction to this miracle is not one of prostrate humility but of rage and hate.

While Oskar does not clarify the reasons for his hatred, we are able to arrive at an explanation through an examination of his character. Oskar defines himself as neither a good nor evil person but as a mixture of the two. His inner make-up contains elements of Rasputin and Goethe, Apollo and Dionysos. It is therefore unthinkable for Oskar to worship a god who stands for only the good element in the world. Here Grass aligns himself with a school of thought that sees the need for a new religion. Such writers as C.G. Jung and Hermann Hesse claim that the Christian Deity is not adequate for our times, for He represents only that half of the world that is good, pure, and noble. The other evil half, assigned to Satan, is denied. A religion truly representative of the world, however, should venerate and sanctify everything. So in addition to the worship of God, we also need a service of Satan. It is probably in reference to this that Oskar breaks Four lightbulbs on his return home: the Father, the Son, the Holy Ghost, and Satan.

Grass' Jesus signifies his agreement with this way of thinking when He appoints Oskar as His successor. The miracle itself is nothing less than an affirmation of the duality of Oskar's divinity. Nevertheless, Oskar's actions show that he is not an atheist but a believer. While he rejects Christ and everything He stands for, Oskar does not refuse the commission to serve as the foundation of the new Church. He takes to hanging around the Church and even lets himself be locked up overnight in the hope that Jesus will tell him exactly how he should proceed as the new Messiah.

Historical Allusions: Oskar's return home gives rise to difficulties with the Board of Health. During the latter period of the war, a program was inaugurated to weed out biological impurities. Since Oskar was regarded as a malformed dwarf, the government put pressure on Matzerath to have Oskar sent away to an extermination camp. When his father refused, the surprised Oskar shows his gratitude by admitting to himself the possibility that Matzerath is indeed his real father and thereafter occasionally refers to himself as Oskar Matzerath.

CHAPTER THIRTEEN: THE DUSTERS

Title: During the last year of the war, numerous armed gangs of youths emerged throughout Germany. Specializing in robbery, mugging and rape, they gave the police a great deal of trouble. The Dusters take their name from the painful way they dig their knuckles into the victim's muscles just above the elbow.

Historical Analogy: The heedless destruction of the war is now reflected in the way Oskar uses his voice. Formerly, he made use of his gift only as a means of protest or to protect his drum from adults. Now he breaks glass from pure malice.

Enraged at finding the church locked one evening, Oskar expresses his hostility by the wanton destruction of street lamps. Thus, destruction for its own sake coincides with the Dusters' viewpoint.

Theme And Characterization: Returning home from the church one evening, Oskar is intercepted by the Dusters. Oskar introduces himself as Jesus and gains their confidence and admiration by performing a "miracle" which in this case consists in demolishing all the glass in a chocolate factory. Impressed, the gang appoints Oskar its new leader. The manner in which authority is transferred is significant. The leadership of the gang automatically reverts from Stortebeker to Oskar because the Dusters fall under the spell of Oskar's charisma. The symbol of authority is the wristwatch which Oskar symbolically accepts but immediately hands over to Firestealer. Thus Oskar the Messiah gathers a band of disciples. Their actions, however, are anything but Christian.

The Duster's destructiveness is not ideologically motivated; neither can it be defined as a form of protest. They are against everything. Robbing, stealing, and raping with the aid of Oskar's voice, they regard their actions as an end in themselves. Appropriately, their own acts of violence are merely a reflection of the officially sanctioned mayhem, genocide, and wholesale slaughter. Even when the gang is caught and brought to trial, no one expresses remorse.

CHAPTER FOURTEEN: THE CHRISTMAS PLAY

Title: The title of this chapter is a euphemism for the *Black Mass* performed by Oskar and the Dusters at Christmas.

Theme And Characterization: Grass continues to develop his religious **theme**. As the gang's leader Oskar aids them in their exploits. His first action is to order the burial of tommy guns, handgrenades, and other weapons, pointing out "Our weapons are of a different kind." This is a reference to a similar remark made by Jesus. As it turns out, Oskar's glass-shattering voice is the different kind of weapon that enables the Dusters to enter various buildings. Oskar also uses his voice to wreak vengeance on schoolteachers who have incurred the Duster's displeasure. The similarity between the effects of Oskar's long-range voice and the wrath of God is unmistakable.

In addition, parallels to the New Testament abound. For instance, new members initiated into the gang must swear allegiance by placing their hands on Oskar's drum, a substitute Bible. The Duster's headquarters is decorated with religious paraphernalia looted from churches. And finally, as in the days of pre-Christian Rome, the new sect must hold its meetings at night and in secret.

The New Messiah: Oskar's glorification as the new Messiah takes place on the night of December 18, 1944. On this date the Dusters break into the Church of the Sacred Heart, sever the boy Jesus from the Virgin's thigh, and put Oskar in his place. The presence of the Holy Ghost in the ceremony that is to follow is symbolized by the red-beamed flashlights illuminating Oskar on his perch. Three of the Dusters offer Mass, not to God, but to Oskar whose drum, providing a running commentary, captures the faith of the congregation. The high point is reached when they recite the Lord's Prayer to Oskar.

When arrival of the police disrupts the meeting, it is learned that Lucy Rennwand has betrayed the group to the civil authorities. The terminology used to describe her indicates that she is meant to be regarded not only as the modern Judas but also as the personification of the Satanic elements in human nature. As the new Deity who combines within himself both the good and the diabolical, Oskar appropriately bestows his approval on her actions which he does by symbolically offering her something to eat.

Yet Oskar is not prepared to emulate Christ in every respect, such as suffering the consequences of his actions. Unlike the Biblical Christ whose disciples escape punishment by claiming they do not know Him, Oskar goes free by denying his disciples. Taking refuge behind his three-year-old stature, the police naturally assume that the gang was using him for some sinister, occult ritual.

Historical Events: These events coincide with Germany's desperate military situation. Again, conditions are conveyed not through description but through the use of certain phrases that made their way into the language toward the end of the war. The references to "secret weapons," "final victory," and "Rundstedt's Offensive" (The Battle of the Bulge) call forth vivid memories for any German reader alive at the time. Oskar uses a syntactical device to draw attention to the Russian advance on East Prussia. One member of the gang, Moorkanne, is an excellent student at the high school who has a good chance of passing his examinations brilliantly if, says Oskar, "the Russian Army should raise no objections."

Parody Of *Novel Of Education*: In Goethe's *Wilhelm Master's Travels*, a small group of people set up a "Pedagogical Province" where they strive to live according to the principles of virtue and wisdom, educating their children in the same values. Grass parodies this ethical utopia by drawing a parallel to the Duster's headquarters. They have furnished it with stolen religious objects, and there they practice an ethical code that its members consider superior to those of society. When confronted with the absurdity of their actions and the **theme** of the inconclusiveness of life, the optimism inherent in the *Novel of Education* is both defeated and trivialized.

CHAPTER FIFTEEN: THE ANT TRAIL

Title: Towards the end of the chapter, a trail of ants is forced to make a detour around Matzerath's dead body.

Theme And Characterization: This chapter deals with two themes: First, the events of Oskar's trial, and second, the Russian occupation of Danzig. Oskar denies himself the opportunity to describe the Dusters' trial in the traditional way. He avoids articulate counsels for the defense, weeping witnesses, or wrathful public prosecutors. The suicidal plunge of each gang member from a thirty-two foot tower into the empty swimming pool is a **metaphor** for confession and sentencing. Even though each youth hesitates at the top of the tower he is forced to jump through Lucy Rennwand's testimony. Oskar does not see her as the skinny girl with the triangular face, but as a malicious witch perched on Satan's knee. In a veiled reference to Satan's temptation of Christ on the tower, Lucy-Satan urges Oskar-Jesus to take the plunge. Oskar's decision to climb back down the tower without jumping signifies his refusal of the temptation.

Although the Dusters' punishment is not specified, the leap from the thirty-two foot tower into the empty swimming pool clearly indicates that most are to be executed.

Grass encountered a difficult aesthetic problem when he set about describing the Russian occupation of Danzig. Following the war, innumerable books were published that recounted the horrors of the occupation troops. Most writers employed the same technique of detailed personal narrative; they vied with each other to relate the most gruesome and shocking experience. By the late 1950s, readers had grown weary of the accounts. Grass solves the problem by describing in a few short paragraphs the meeting between three Russian soldiers and Oskar's family.

Oskar's Guilt: To the list of deaths which Oskar has indirectly caused is now added a death for which he is directly responsible. In the cellar Matzerath suddenly realizes that he is still wearing his Nazi Party pin. Wishing to hide his affiliation with the Nazis, he throws it on the floor where Oskar retrieves it. When the Russians enter, Oskar first thinks about pinning it on Matzerath's back, but then hands it to him. Matzerath pops the pin in his mouth with a view to swallowing it but gags. His hysterical gyrations frighten the Kalmuck who shoots him. Much later in the novel Oskar admits that he opened the clasp because he suspected that his father would try to swallow it.

The reasons Oskar wishes his father's death are clear. He has always hated him for claiming to be his father, and he roundly despises his unthinking way of life. Oskar particularly resents his father for stealing Maria whom Oskar still loves. Most of all, Oskar will not forgive him for finally sending the letter which will commit him to an institution. Even though Oskar will later suffer intensely from guilt, he will never really regret his actions.

Historical Analogy: Matzerath's death is Grass' way of depicting the end of the Hitler era. His frantic death throes symbolize the last ridiculous struggle of the Nazis.

CHAPTER SIXTEEN: SHOULD I OR SHOULDN'T I

Title: Here the title refers to Oskar's debate whether he should or should not throw his last drum into Matzerath's grave.

Historical Analogy: Even though Grass treats the arrival of the Russians casually, his long and detailed discourse on Danzig's past throws the present circumstances into perspective. In the light of history, it can be seen that one more invasion does not count for much. In his cynicism Grass again demonstrates his view that the only way to adequately reflect recent history is through images.

Historical Background: In 1945 the Russians handed Danzig over to Poland with the agreement between the two countries that all German nationals would be returned to Germany and that Polish citizens would assume ownership of the vacated German property: an arrangement that would partially recompensate Poland for Polish territory annexed by Russia. Mr. Fajngold, a Jew from Galicia, is one of the many sent into Danzig.

Characterization: Fajngold appears unannounced one day to take possession of the family grocery store. His incredible hardships, however, have unhinged his mind, so he still imagines that his large family is with him even though he witnessed their death in the Treblinka extermination camp. Although he was able to survive because he was employed as disinfector, he has a psychological attachment to disinfectant as the only stable object in a chaotic world. His chief trait is the impulse to disinfect everything and everyone.

Theme: The chief theme of this chapter is Oskar's guilt. As he accompanies Matzerath's funeral cortege to Saspe and watches while the grave is dug, he debates whether he should throw his drum in with the coffin. Flicking stones at an iron wreath he asks "Should I or shouldn't I," much like a young girl plucking petals from a daisy would say "He loves me, he loves me not." This scene conveys Oskar's complete callousness and irresponsibility.

Regarding the drum as a symbol of his guilt, he believes that he can free himself of responsibility by burying the symbol. Paradoxically, however, he merely exchanges one symbol for another: his drum for a hump. The fact that he immediately begins to grow, and undergoes a grotesque metamorphosis, signifies that no one can escape guilt. of the two. Viewed in this way, the existence of evil in the world is rendered comprehensible and, therefore, in a way, acceptable. Thus the great fallacy in the Christian interpretation of things is illuminated. Instead of viewing the cosmos as composed of antithetical polarities constantly at war with one another, we should view it as a unity composed of both good and evil.

Historical **Parody**: Once again in the present, we learn that Oskar has grown from three feet to four feet and one inch, is chicken breasted, has a hump, and a head grotesquely large. He is now too tall to pass for a midget or a dwarf and too small to fit into the adult world. His illness and growth is a **parody** of recent German history. His maturity, like that of West Germany, is obtained at the expense of youthful vitality and through acquisition of guilt.

CHAPTER EIGHTEEN: GROWTH IN A FREIGHT CAR

Title: The title defines Oskar's chief occupation during the journey to West Germany.

Historical Background: In June, 1945 the first trains loaded with expelled German nationals left the Eastern provinces. German citizens were herded into freight cars and shipped west. The trip took about three weeks owing to delays and plundering by armed gangs of so-called partisans. During the warm months, many survived the journey. In the terrible winter of 1946–47, however, the expatriates died by the thousands. Polish and Russian authorities, however, looked upon the sufferings with indifference for German atrocities against conquered nations were still fresh in their minds.

Theme And Characterization: When Oskar begins to describe the events in this chapter, his fingers swell so that he can neither write nor drum. At this point the author confirms what the reader has suspected for some time. Oskar is not merely remembering and recording events of the past, he is reliving them with all the vividness of reality. Almost ten years have elapsed since he began to grow in the freight car, yet his fingers still swell in sympathetic response.

Unable to write this chapter himself, Oskar hands the job over to Bruno. The resulting change of narration and style permits us to view Oskar from another perspective. What we see now is a highly intelligent though lazy and condescending individual whose mind seldom dwells in the present.

Again, the chief aim of this chapter is Oskar's guilt. Here it takes the form of painful, misshapen growth. His joints swell, he aches everywhere, and he runs a high fever. The young girl Regina Raeck, who bears an unmistakable resemblance to Lucy Rennwand's triangular fox face, personifies the forces of retribution, guilt, and fear. Her departure at Schwerin provokes an attack of fever and delirium in which Oskar demands to expiate his guilt by jumping from a thirty-two foot swimming tower into an empty pool.

In addition, Oskar's misshapen growth is accompanied by the loss of his glass-shattering voice. As a symbol of innocence, purity, and chastity, the loss of his gift is appropriate, for it should be among the first visible changes.

Domination Of Objects: Here Grass gives another indication of his belief that the course of men's lives is determined by objects - objects that appear to be endowed with a will or force entirely independent of the owner. This is brought out when a group of partisans enter the freight car to loot the travelers' belongings. When the social democrat loquaciously refuses to comply, a partisan kicks him in the stomach with a hobnailed boot formerly the property of the German Army. From the description it is clear that the fault lies not so much in the wearer but in the boots themselves. Grass appears to be saying

Oskar As Christ Figure: The eccentric but remarkably intuitive Leo Schugger is the first to notice the growth. Like Roswitha Raguna, he has the capacity to look into a person's soul and see what is there. A grotesque prophet proclaiming the Messiah, Leo screams that he has "seen the Lord." His shrieks and frenzied behavior, however, frighten the two Russian guards who kill him.

CHAPTER SEVENTEEN: DISINFECTANT

Title: This title defines Mr. Fajngold's view that disinfectant is more important than life.

Theme And Characterization: Just when we feel that we have understood the reasons for Oskar's growth, Grass adds information that casts everything into doubt. We learn that the moment Oskar threw his drum into Matzerath's half-filled grave, Kurt threw a stone which struck Oskar in the back of the head, toppling him into the grave. Although Oskar insists that to grow was his own decision, we cannot be sure.

Oskar compares his illness and high fever metaphorically to a merry-go-round. He, along with four thousand other children killed on an evacuation train, are forced by God to ride the merry-go-round. When the turn is up, He reaches into His pocket and pays for another enforced ride. This is Oskar's way of posing the eternal question: Why does God permit such senseless suffering in the world? If God is beautiful, kind, noble, and just, then how can He allow such madness to prevail? The question is answered in images. For instance, in Oskar's dream, God becomes Rasputin, then Goethe. We recall that Rasputin represents not only the raw, savage, untamed nature but also the diabolical, evil element in human nature. Goethe, on the other hand, signifies everything that is noble, rational, and sublime: the forces of good. But when God changes into one and then into the other, He is defining His dual nature. God is not wholly good or wholly evil, but a combination that anyone who dons German hobnailed boots will be forced to act in accordance with the function for which they were designed, that is, to step on someone. Other instances in which objects dominate lives are the figurehead Niobe, the food Matzerath cooks, the drum Oskar beats, and the pillboxes on the Atlantic wall.

THE TIN DRUM

BOOK THREE

. . . .

CHAPTER ONE: FIRESTONES AND TOMBSTONES

Title: "Firestones" is the literal translation of German Feuersteine, meaning flints. These, Kurt sells on the black market; by contrast, Oskar cuts inscriptions on tombstones.

Historical Background: Between the end of the war and the currency reform in 1948, barter (especially American cigarettes) became the chief medium of exchange. On the flourishing black market a package of Lucky Strikes had the purchasing power of about one hundred dollars. As a result, several new jargonistic words made their way into the language about this time. Using them frequently, the author creates an authentic historical atmosphere.

Theme And Characterization: Now in Dusseldorf, Maria and Kurt are involved in the black market, much to the objection of sister Guste. Described as fat and slow-witted, she objects to black marketeering on moral grounds; nonetheless, she is only too willing to drink the illegally acquired coffee and grow fatter on the black market goodies.

We are surprised to learn that Oskar has given up all pretenses of being a child. He now speaks and acts as an adult. Because this occurs without any explanation or comment, the change is likely to go unobserved by the reader. The reason, of course, is that Oskar can no longer hide behind the physique of a three-year-old child. He further hints that he equates his deformed body and the loss of his glass-shattering voice with his loss of happiness.

Now for the first time Oskar is overcome by an intense longing for happiness. Partially in response to Maria's nagging, but chiefly in search of happiness, Oskar apprentices himself to Korneff the stonecutter. He soon discovers, however, that true happiness probably does not exist outside the imagination and that man must be satisfied with substitute happiness. Nevertheless, Oskar finds contentment engraving messages on tombstones, an ersatz for his drum. Oskar's long disquisition on the search for ersatz happiness, contentment, and satisfaction advance the view that true happiness can be experienced only in the pursuit of that happiness.

Autobiographical Elements: Beginning with this chapter, autobiographical elements play an increasingly important role in the novel. Like his hero, Grass came to Dusseldorf after the war and, while waiting for the new art academy to open, he worked in a monument factory.

CHAPTER TWO: FORTUNA NORTH

Title: Fortuna North is the name of a huge generating facility in the Rhine valley. Near the plant Oskar decides to propose to Maria.

Theme And Characterization: The theme of this chapter deals with subtle changes in Oskar's character. Until now he had rejected the grown-up world and was perfectly content to be just Oskar the child drummer-boy. Now that he has become an adult, however, he is somewhat disconcerted to discover a desire to be not only a part of the adult world but to be acceptable to it. To be sure, he pretends indifference, but it is clear that he does so to avoid being hurt. We may point to specific instances that illuminate these changes. Posing before a mirror in new clothes, Oskar experiences those feelings familiar to every young man who puts on his first new suit. Furthermore, the traditionally heretofore composed Oskar finds himself suddenly susceptible to youthful excitement and to taking pride in his personal appearance.

On the occasion of his first date, Oskar is deeply wounded by Sister Gertrude who accepts his invitation partly from boredom and partly because he has a lot of pastry ration cards. Lacking perception, she suggests an evening of dancing. Although Oskar is used to the eyebrow-lifting and stares, the obviously weird figure they cut on the dance floor is too much for Gertrude. She heads for the door, abandoning Oskar to the applause and curiosity. Oskar's true feelings are concealed in harmless actions, and to show his aplomb he orders straight schnapps and "pretends" to smile.

Nevertheless, Oskar's dancing and his determination to ignore his misshapen body make him a favorite at the Lion's Den. Now that he begins to go there frequently, he reveals his sudden need for companionship. It is also Oskar's need of human company that leads him to propose marriage to Maria. Before doing so, however, he first goes through a strange purification ritual to make him worthy of Maria's hand. He gives up his visits to the Lion's Den and breaks his connection with the girls at the telephone company.

Oskar is not disappointed by Maria's refusal. Again, his true feelings are conveyed through a syntactical device. Her refusal is placed almost as an afterthought at the end of a long, involved sixty-word sentence of the type for which the German language is so well known. Fortunately, this and other similar syntactical stratagems have been well rendered by the translator and so can be appreciated by the English reading student.

CHAPTER THREE: MADONNA 49

Title: This chapter takes its title from the portrait painted of Oskar and Ulla as Madonna and child. The year is 1949.

Theme And Characterization: The theme of this chapter is concerned with the different ways Oskar's character is seen by the students at the art academy. If it is true that the genuine artist has the ability to look inside his subject and bring his inmost nature to the surface in the portrait, then we may conclude that most of the students at the academy should be in a different business.

They illuminate Oskar as a "condemnation of humanity" or as the evil reflection of the war. In their eagerness to portray the evil element in human nature and to draw cogent parallels to recent history, they fail to see beneath Oskar's diabolical, Rasputin exterior. Since Oskar's other side (the Goethean, represented by his blue eyes) remains unseen, the artists never succeed in turning out a truly perceptive likeness.

Oskar As A Christ Figure: It is the artist Raskolnikov who perceives Oskar's true self. So named because he is always preoccupied with the problem of crime and punishment or guilt and redemption, it is appropriate that Raskolnikov should discern what the others have failed to see: Oskar's guilt and Oskar's divinity.

From the beginning, he intuitively senses that Oskar as a model is somehow incomplete, for Oskar's guilt is not portrayed. After a few attempts, the artist discovers that a tin drum is the appropriate symbol. Oskar's frantic objections are overcome by Raskolnikov's assertions that guilt always returns. Now that all the missing parts are in place, the artist paints his masterpiece, Madonna 49. The picture shows Oskar sitting on Ulla's right thigh, she as the Madonna, he as Jesus the drummer boy. Both are nude. Unknown to Raskolnikov, he has painted an exact replica of the scene played out five years earlier in the Church of the Sacred Heart.

Ulla The Muse: During Carnival, Oskar attends the annual artist's ball where he meets Corporal Lankes, now a struggling young artist, who introduces him to his girlfriend Ulla. Oskar immediately nicknames her Ulla the Muse and, as the events unfold, her nickname proves to be apt. She is one of those rare individuals whose mere presence brings out the creative impulse in men. She inspires artists in different ways: Lankes finds he can work best after slapping her around. Raskolnikov stares at her nude body and talks of crime and punishment. Ulla herself is merely a vacuous, scatterbrained nymph who regards her modeling as an artistic creation.

CHAPTER FOUR: THE HEDGEHOG

Title: Oskar's new landlord bears a resemblance to a hedgehog.

Historical Background: Oskar's new quarters in Zeidler's house reflect the housing shortage in the years after the war. The situation was so acute that people were forced to pay exorbitant prices for the privilege of living beneath the eaves or in the cellar. Oskar's room is a converted toilet which he rents solely because it is next door to a nurse, Sister Dorothea.

Theme: Oskar suffers from a fixation on nurses. Although he never sees Sister Dorothea, he falls in love with her merely because she is a nurse. He reads her mail, listens for her footstep when she returns home at night, and loses himself in a lover's fantasy. Oskar's discourse on nurses and his feelings for Sister Dorothea, which occupy the greater portion of this chapter, reveal his capacity for self-scrutiny and self-judgment. Oskar hides nothing from himself. This is clear from the frequent shifts from first-person narrative to third. In a way, Oskar enjoys stepping outside himself to have a look at himself.

Characterization: Grass is a master of characterization. His portrait of Zeidler the landlord provides the reader with a vivid image. Here his technique consists of two parts. First, he describes in a few words the subject's exterior morphology. In the case of Zeidler, we learn that he is fat, squat, hairy, and uncouth. Then Grass confronts the more difficult problem of portraying his character. In the present case, he wishes to paint Zeidler as a self-important, cretinous nobody. He accomplishes this by associating him with an object, the rugs, that is in itself insignificant. Through constant repetition, the object becomes an integral part of his character and when appended to any statement, renders both it and the individual absurd.

CHAPTER FIVE: IN THE CLOTHES CUPBOARD

Title: This chapter takes its name from the clothes cupboard in Sister Dorothea's room in which Oskar takes a journey through the past.

Satire: Grass the former artist is visible behind the vicious characterization of Ulla and her friends. Thrown out by Lankes, Ulla lives with one phony artist-type after another. She adds to her vocabulary such high-sounding but empty phrases as dynamic atomism, granular perspective, and constellated accents. This pseudo, artsy-craftsy mumbo-jumbo is the author's way of satirizing the barrenness of some modern art.

Theme And Characterization: One day, Sister Dorothea forgets to lock her door and Oskar goes in for a look, finally crawling inside her clothes cupboard. Here, in the ersatz security of his Grandmother's skirts, he discovers the organizing principle of thought which he later uses to write the account of his life. Feeling about in the darkness, he finds a green, patent leather belt which immediately reminds him of the shiny green eels (in the chapter "Good Friday Fare"). So vivid is the recollection that he relives the events on the breakwater.

Principle Of Organization: Grass' organization of experience resembles that of Marcel Proust. Memory is conceived as a series of parallel, physical sensations which assume their identity independent of chronological order. Therefore, a physical sensation, such as that of the patent-leather belt, creates in his mind a connection between events widely separated in time. When Oskar beats out a short melody on the cupboard wall, he discovers that the object linking all his past experiences is the drum. Now when Oskar wishes to recall a past event, he need only drum the appropriate melody.

What Oskar smells in the cupboard also serves as an illustration of the organizing principle. The smell of vinegar characteristic of Sister Dorothea calls to mind memories of his other women. It is noteworthy that with the exception of Mrs. Kater, Oskar associates odors only with women who stand in an erotic relationship to him. The scent of vinegar recalls other scents that finally result in a physical release.

CHAPTER SIX: KLEPP

Title: "Klepp" is Oskar's nickname for his friend Egon Munzer.

Characterization: This chapter introduces Klepp who lives at the end of the hallway. He has spent the last several months lying in bed paralyzed by a kind of inertia of the soul. He has his room so arranged that he can do everything (including going to the toilet) without getting up. He claims that this arrangement is an elaborate experiment to determine the state of his health.

Oskar As Christ Figure: One of the characteristics associated with the Messiah is performance of such miracles as healing the lame, curing the sick, and raising the dead. Oskar performs the requisite miracle by raising Klepp from his bed. The frequent textual references to corpses, filth, and the cadaverous stench create an atmosphere of death and decay and show that although Klepp's body is very much alive, his spirit is dead. Oskar performs the miracle with his drum. In the course of drumming, Oskar's story of his life kindles a spark in Klepp's soul. Seizing his flute, the two friends take a nostalgic journey through Oskar's past life. Finally, the words used to describe Klepp's decision to get out of bed, take a bath and start to live indicate that he is meant to be regarded as the modern Lazarus raised from the dead by Oskar, the Messiah. In the Biblical miracle, Christ raised Lazarus' body whereas Oskar breathes life into Klepp's spirit.

CHAPTER SEVEN: ON THE FIBER RUG

Title: The fiber rug refers to Oskar's efforts, as Satan, to seduce Sister Dorothea.

Characterization: Returning to the present, Oskar breaks off his narrative to describe Klepp's personality. This frequently used technique permits both the author and the reader to view the **protagonists** from a different perspective. The device has another, more subtle effect: alienation in the Brechtian sense. Through the constant juxtaposition of past and present, with Oskar acting as narrator as well as Oskar the participant, Oskar prevents himself from becoming lost in his own story. By remaining aloof from his narrative, he insures that he is always in artistic control.

A similar effect is exerted on the reader. The reader is never allowed to forget that he is a reader. Oskar makes sure that his audience is wide awake and critical at all times. The author does not believe that the object of his artistic skill should be to carry his audience to the heights of passion and the depths of sorrow, but to keep it at a distance. The ideal reader should be a sober, objective spectator who, free from illusion, evaluates rationally everything he reads.

Klepp: In some ways, Klepp is a representative of the post-war German. He is a confirmed atheist and Marxist, but if he discovers that a priest possesses a good record collection, he is not above taking communion on Sundays. Jazz and Communism are somehow related in his mind. Klepp's world revolves around jazz and the satiation of his appetite. In fact, he feels that all the problems of humanity can be solved by large portions of blood sausage and onion rings washed down with torrents of beer.

Theme: The theme of Oskar's dual Christ-Satan nature is here further elaborated. After he and Klepp lay the coconut fiber runner in the hallway, Oskar takes a leftover piece into his room. That night when Sister Dorothea comes home, Oskar surprises her in the dark bathroom and, with the aid of the fiber rug, convinces her that he is Satan on a mission of seduction.

Although Sister Dorothea is frantically willing, Oskar is unable to perform. His final humiliation occurs when she packs up and moves out, giving him a final kick in the chest.

Oskar's inability to perform the sex act is connected to his guilt and his loss of innocence. While still a three-year-old and innocent, Oskar encountered no difficulty in satisfying his women. To be sure, he was partially responsible for the death of several people and was guilty of many callous acts, but he was able to transfer that guilt onto his drum or, as he says, to let his innocence grow again. When he buried this symbol in Matzerath's grave, however, the guilt was transferred to his body, manifesting itself in impotence and deformity.

Oskar As Christ Figure: The religious **theme** is also closely connected to Oskar's impotence. As a Christ figure, it is appropriate that he should declare for celibacy. He does so, however, unwillingly, begging the Satanic within him to provide the necessary strength to make love to Sister Dorothea.

At this point in the novel, it has become apparent that Oskar is reluctantly accepting his role as the modern Christ. He resists that side of him and frequently tries to subvert it. We know from the many remarks he makes that he would prefer to spend the remainder of his life in his hospital bed writing, drumming, and receiving visits. In fact, he dreads the day when he has to leave the hospital a free man, for then he will be obliged to gather disciples and commence his mission.

CHAPTER EIGHT: IN THE ONION CELLAR

Title: This heading is taken from the post-war nightspot where Oskar, Klepp, and Scholler work as a jazz trio.

Theme And Characterization: In this chapter Grass satirizes Germany of the 1950s. The sickness of modern German society arises from its materialistic values that are totally rational, allowing no place for the expression of feeling. This is brought out most clearly by the attitudes of the customers who frequent the Onion Cellar. They are victims of a society that sublimates repressed feeling into the pursuit of prosperity and the struggle for material success. It is this institutionalized hedonism, accepted as a substitute for emotional release, that has turned the individual into a stiff, unbending, unfeeling robot.

Here Grass is depicting a basic precept of Western civilization. Beginning with the Age of Reason, men have taught their children that feeling should be subordinated to reason. In the lifelong conflict between what we want to do and what we ought to do, we are told that true happiness can be gained only by obeying the voice of duty. Children are further taught that society frowns upon the expression of anything but the most superficial emotions. "Keeping a stiff upper lip" in the face of adversity is a value held in high esteem in most Western societies. Adjectives such as childish, irrational, and emotionally immature are applied to individuals who give free expression to their feelings. Such epithets in the business and professional world spell immediate ruin.

Grass is saying that feeling should not be stifled, but allowed to expand and realize itself. The effects of systematic emotional repression are well portrayed in Schmuh's clientele. The habitues of the Onion Cellar are mostly over thirty. Coming from many different occupations, they represent a cross-section of modern German society. They all share one thing in common - a need to talk and to weep. Unable to cry of their own accord, they wait for Schmuh to pass round onions which they peel and dice until their eyes are blinded by tears. Thus, hiding behind artificial tears, they are able to weep authentic ones without embarrassment. The communal weeping is accompanied by the recounting of problems, missed opportunities, ruined careers, and stories of alienated children.

Surprisingly, those customers who try to save the cover charge and dice their own onions at home discover that the therapy works only in the Onion Cellar. It appears as if people need an audience to cry before and the comfort of brotherhood engendered through communal weeping.

Adults are not the only patrons of Schmuh's establishment, for Mondays are reserved for students. It is noteworthy that the majority are made up of art and medical students. If it is true that a successful artist requires a good emotional balance, it is not surprising that aspiring artists should frequent Schmuh's cellar. There, they are more acutely aware of the soul-destroying elements in society. Medical students, on the other hand, present the problem in a different light. One of the chief dicta associated with the medical profession warns the doctor to avoid emotional involvement with his patients unless he wants his ability to be impaired. In other words, the student is asked to repress humane feelings in the name of humanity. The element of self-protection also plays a part here. If feelings are not involved, they cannot be hurt. But as the students themselves realize, life consists in more than protecting oneself from pain. The medical students in the Onion Cellar sense that they may be in danger of becoming emotionally sterile.

Schmuh's Orgy: The orgy that Schmuh tries to create by handing round an unheard of second onion is a flop, resulting not in a terrifying emotional outburst but in a distorted, perverse behavior, a further indication of the sad state of the modern soul.

Oskar As Christ Figure: Quite by chance, Oskar discovers a new power within himself. When the orgy threatens to get out of hand, Oskar takes charge of the situation. Playing "with his heart," he learns that he has the magical power to awaken repressed feelings of guilt and fear, to break down inhibitions, and to transport his listeners back to childhood. Their regression to childhood is complete when all of them symbolically wet their pants.

CHAPTER NINE: ON THE ATLANTIC WALL OR CONCRETE ETERNAL

Title: In this particular instance the literal translation of the original German title is more revealing: "On the Atlantic Wall, or The Bunkers Can't Get Rid of Their Concrete." The implication is that the bunkers and pillboxes will be there until the crack of doom.

Schmuh's Death: The war-torn society has now become the affluent society. Even though basic needs remain the same, the first signs of boredom and jaded tastes appear. The decline of Schmuh's popularity and his death reflect the growing demand for more sophisticated entertainment. Following the evening of wet pants, the guests will have nothing to do with onions, demanding Oskar's drum instead. Depressed at the decline of his importance, Schmuh raises his spirits by shooting sparrows. Schmuh's falling popularity is reflected in the violation of his self-imposed sparrow code. He has never shot more than twelve birds at one time - that would be wasteful. The day he shoots a thirteenth purely for the pleasure of watching it fall, he is killed in an auto accident brought about by thousands of swarming sparrows.

Theme And Characterization: Oskar examines from a different angle certain scenes from the chapter "Mystical, Barbaric, Bored.

" We recall that at that time Corporal Lankes indifferently machine-gunned seven nuns on orders from Lieutenant Herzog. If the decision had been up to him, he would not have killed them. How Lankes would have acted is demonstrated in this chapter when the nuns appear once again. He lures the pretty, young Sister Agneta into the pillbox, where he and Oskar are living, and seduces her. Afterwards, Lankes stretches out in the sand and nonchalantly listens as Oskar describes her suicide in the surf. The drowning nun, however, simply fires Lankes' artistic imagination and provides him with excellent subject matter for a series of paintings based on drowning nuns.

This **episode** gives Grass' views on the villainy of war criminals. Lankes is mean, selfish, and brutal. Yet he is far from sadistic; he is not attracted by bloodshed. Neither is he insensitive, for he excels in a profession that places a high premium on sensitivity. Grass is saying here that social crimes are committed much like war crimes: indifferently and callously.

CHAPTER TEN: THE RING FINGER

Title: The human finger, sporting a ring, that Oskar's rented dog finds becomes the symbol of Oskar's atonement.

Theme And Characterization: This chapter shows how the reluctant Oskar is gradually drawn ever further into the Christ role. When Doctor Dosch first approaches Oskar about the possibility of appearing on stage with his drum, his first reaction is to quit thinking about it and go on a vacation. Later when he tries to destroy the idea by tearing up the calling card, he finds that he cannot forget the telephone number. Significantly, his decision to call on Doctor Dosch is dictated not by curiosity nor by an impulse to fulfill a mission but by simple financial necessity.

The West Concert Agency is lodged in a gleaming new office tower. It is here on the eighth floor that Oskar, the new Messiah, is tempted to sell his powers for money. Unlike Christ's indignant refusals, Oskar signs on the dotted line. As it turns out, the owner of the agency is Bebra who now appears as the omniscient and accusing Father Confessor. Oskar's confession of his part in the deaths of his mother and father, Jan and Roswitha, exemplifies a symbolic purification which is to prepare him for his new career.

Although both Oskar and Bebra play parts with solemn dignity, neither takes the scene seriously. For instance, even as Oskar covers his face and pleads for mercy, he is thinking meanwhile that this pose displays his beautiful hands to the best advantage. A ruse sure to awaken Bebra's sympathy. Forgiveness, however, is forthcoming only after Oskar signs the contract.

The New Messiah: If Christ had waited until the twentieth century to preach his gospel, he probably would have encountered a fate similar to Oskar's. Now in the hands of Bebra's formidable advertising machine, the new Messiah finds that he has suddenly become a commodity, a hot consumer-item to be dressed in a flashy package and sold at a fancy price. All over Germany he is billed as a prophet and seer, a healer of body and soul. Before long, he is built up into a cult figure pursued by throngs of old people who want to touch him. He even turns atheists and blasphemers into believers and churchgoers, thereby earning favorable reviews from the religious press.

A characteristic associated with the Biblical Christ is that of poverty. Although Oskar earns a fortune, he makes little use of it; he continues to live in the converted bathroom and dresses poorly. Furthermore, he is indifferent to the lawsuit resulting from a breach of contract although by ignoring it he loses a great deal of money.

The structure of Oskar's performance is simple. By playing different rhythms on his drum, he is able to transport his listeners back to childhood and makes them relive any sensation he chooses. Oskar's magical power affects everyone, but especially the very old. That is, those most susceptible to nostalgia, those who regret a misspent youth, those who seek to recapture the happiness and innocence of childhood.

Black Witch: Of the many melodies in Oskar's repertoire, his favorite is "The Black Witch" (Die Schwarze Kochin). Reducing fear and guilt to their rhythmical components, he plays the song to an audience of tough coal-miners whose dangerous occupation should have inured them against fear. Yet Oskar reduces the hardened men to tears and cries of terror that demolish all the glass in the theater. By so doing, Oskar finds a surrogate for his own lost vocal powers.

Grass uses "The Black Witch" as a universal symbol of fear and guilt taken from the well-known German children's song of the same name. On the surface, the song appears quite harmless. As a group of children march round in a clockwise circle, suddenly one child, singing the words, breaks away and marches in the opposite direction. Each time he completes a full circle, he chooses one of the children to join him in the outside ring until there is only one child remaining in the center. This child covers his face with his hands, pretending shame, while the others shout, "Pfui, Pfui, Pfui." The children, of course, are unaware of the game's highly symbolic nature. In a way, the remaining child has assumed the role of scapegoat. The frustrating and terrifying element here is that although the child is innocent, he is singled out as bearer of great guilt. This ritual, along with its implications of guilt, reappears in various disguises throughout the novel. In this chapter, for example, Oskar's behavior during the first interview with Bebra is a veiled reenactment of the song. While

Bebra chants the circumstances of Oskar's guilt, Oskar covers his face with his hands, pretending shame. Oskar, however, takes special care to let the reader know that he is pretending.

Ring Finger: The **episode** of the ring finger illustrates Grass' organization technique. From the chapter's title, the reader expects to hear a great deal about a ring finger. Paradoxically, this is not the case. The main body of this chapter deals with Oskar's meeting with Bebra and his role as a celebrity. Only toward the end is the heading clarified. The following chapter, despite its heading defines the circumstances of the ring finger and the role that it will play in Oskar's fate.

CHAPTER ELEVEN: THE LAST STREETCAR OR ADORATION OF A PRESERVING JAR

Title: The title refers to the two chief **themes** developed in this chapter. The last streetcar is supposed to be Victor Weluhn's last ride before execution. The second part of the heading describes Oskar's worship of the ring finger preserved in alcohol.

Theme: Oskar, sensing that the ring finger found by Lux belongs to Sister Dorothea, preserves it in a fruit jar of alcohol and worships it as a saint's relic. A careful reading of Oskar's prayer to the finger indicates that he prays for forgiveness and deliverance from the Black Witch.

Victor Weluhn: Late one night when Oskar and Vittlar borrow a streetcar for a joy ride, they pick up two men dragging Victor Weluhn. We remember that Victor Weluhn had managed to escape during the battle of the Polish Post Office September 1, 1939. In October of that year a warrant was issued for his execution. Now twelve years later the two men assigned to tracking him down have done so and intend to carry out the order to eliminate him.

The very idea that such an order could still be valid, or even considered valid in 1951, is Grass' way of showing Germany's failure to come to terms with its past. The two men are unable to see a distinction between the present state of affairs and those of the past. They answer every argument with the fanatical "an order is an order," a statement which bears witness to the evil inherent in the unquestioning obedience of subjects submitting to the authority characteristic of the German military. The corrupted principle of obedience, Grass believes, was in large part responsible for both world wars.

Oskar As Christ Figure: Oskar saves Victor Weluhn by performing another miracle, thereby fulfilling an additional requirement of a Christ figure. At the moment Weluhn is to be executed, Oskar conjures up a squadron of Polish cavalry who carry him to safety.

Vittlar's Testimony: The main portion of this chapter consists of a copy of Vittlar's testimony to the court. This narrative technique serves not only to advance the story but also to provide the reader with a different point of view. Grass changes his style so well that it actually appears as though the piece were written by another person. (The change of style is somewhat less apparent in the translation.)

Vittlar's testimony, however, tells us more about Vittlar than about Oskar. Bored with life, he is delighted to follow Oskar about Germany on his tours. When he complains that it is difficult for him to live in the shadow of Oskar's fame the two friends concoct a scheme that will bring Vittlar instant fame. Vittlar will provide the necessary circumstantial evidence to convict Oskar of Sister

Dorothea's murder and Oskar will lend credence to the accusation by pretending to flee the country. Thus, at the end of the novel, the reader learns the details of the mysterious trial mentioned in the first chapter that has confined Oskar in a mental institution.

CHAPTER TWELVE: THIRTY

Title: Oskar ends his narrative on his thirtieth birthday. ("Thirty," in editorial jargon, also indicates "the end of the manuscript.")

Theme And Characterization: To lend credence to his guilt, Oskar flees by train to Paris. If his flight is to be convincing both to himself and to the authorities, then he must pretend that he is fleeing something or at least try to scare himself so that he will look guilty and frightened when the Interpol detectives arrest him. While he is casting about for a suitable object of fear, the rhythm of the wheels on the steel tracks suddenly reminds him of the children's song "The Black Witch." Until this point he had never feared the witch, and had resisted her at every point. But as his guilt grows, his fear of her increases. Once he has let her under his skin, he is tortured by a delirium of accumulated guilt. The witch, he realizes, is not only omnipresent, but she has been and always will be present. She lurked in darkened doorways, attended the plundering of Sigismund Markus' toyshop, she sang when the street urchins brewed the foul soup, and became flesh and blood in Lucy Renwand's triangular fox face. Thus, she is universal; she points an accusing finger at everyone. Especially Oskar. The rhythm of the wheels suggests the song's words: "You are guilty, and you are guilty, and you most of all."

Oskar is disappointed that he is not arrested at the train station for this means that he will have to make an effort to fall into the hands of the police. He takes the Metro to Orly airport and gets off at the last station but one, correctly assuming the police will be waiting there rather than at the end station. Oskar ascends the escalator at the Maison Blanche station ("white" for innocence) and turns himself over to the police. And he does so joyfully. Both his flight and symbolic ascent from the Metro Underworld are described in terms indicating that Oskar views his capture and forthcoming imprisonment as a release from guilt. Innocent of the crime of which he is accused, he can regard his unjust imprisonment as an opportunity to atone his real crimes.

Oskar As Christ Figure: Oskar ascends the escalator and announces in three languages, to the detectives waiting at the top, "I am Jesus." Oskar narrates these events on his thirtieth birthday, an occasion that he has dreaded for years. His chief fear is that the real murderer will be found, the case reopened, and the judge find him innocent. Consequently, he will be flung out into the streets and, like Christ, be obliged to gather disciples around himself and his drum.

We can therefore understand Oskar's negative attitude when his lawyer bursts into the room with the news that his case has been reopened. Most of all, Oskar will miss his hospital bed and its innocent-white security because he must leave them and confront the wicked witch who is waiting outside.

THE TIN DRUM

CHARACTER ANALYSIS

....

BEBRA

Bebra is an undeveloped **protagonist** who functions as Oskar's omniscient master and teacher. When they first meet, Bebra immediately knows why Oscar had refused not to grow. Like the other midgets and eccentrics in the novel, Bebra is endowed with the power to foretell the future. He tells Oskar that difficult times are ahead and that it will be especially dangerous for the little people. Consequently, he advises Oskar to take up politics so that he can always be on the Rostrum rather than in front of it.

Bebra is also used as a means for indirectly reflecting the course of the war. As the military situation worsens, the need for effective propaganda increases. Thus when he reappears in Danzig in 1944, he wears captain's uniform and has a chauffeured limousine at his disposal. Bebra's talent for survival lies in his ability to adapt to any situation. While at the front he intersperses his act with such appropriate phrases as "final Victory," "Secret Weapons," and "for the glory of the Greater German Reich." Later in West Germany he takes advantage of the need for entertainment to amass a fortune.

When he interviews Oskar as the owner of the West Concert Agency, he appears as both the father-confessor and the archetypal judge figure who dispenses absolution and retribution in accordance with the accepted modern usage: he requires Oskar to sign a contract.

JAN BRONSKI

Jan Bronski is the suave and handsome lover of Agnes and Oskar's presumptive father. His whole life revolves around stimulation of the senses. He dresses expensively in the latest fashion, uses cologne, and smokes foreign cigarettes with a sophisticated flair. His affair with Agnes is characterized as "the appetite that is never satisfied." The two meet in a hotel room on Thursdays to enjoy an afternoon of lovemaking and they continue the caresses at home under the card table, furtively on the sofa, and more passionately in the bedroom.

Despite Jan's boldness in matters of love, he is basically shy and withdrawn, the archetypal civilian. This is brought out most clearly in the battle for the Polish Post Office, when he approaches the post office expecting to be turned back. Yet precisely because of his fine civilian clothes, the soldiers permit him to enter. Inside the building, he is rendered useless as a fighter through his highly developed sensitivity. During the battle itself Jan's actions appear to be those of a coward; he screams, shrieks, and weeps hysterically at every bursting shell. We realize, however, on closer examination that he experiences war on a different level than do most men. This is apparent when his actions are compared to Kobyella's. Kobyella thrives on war. The battle transforms him from a meek janitor into a bloodthirsty killer. Indeed, he seems to draw strength from the exploding shells. Jan, on the other hand, experiences war spiritually. Each explosion, regardless of its intended victim, wounds his soul. Jan's extreme sensitivity does allow him to achieve a kind of victory over his death. If it is true that the chief object of an execution is to subject the prisoner to a final period of extreme mental agony, then Jan escapes this torture for his mind by then is so deranged that he no longer understands what is happening to him. Consequently, he faces the firing squad with the same foolish smile that he showed on the newsreels.

BRUNO

Bruno is Oskar's keeper. Eccentric and somewhat obtuse, he receives inspiration only from the ceiling. Nevertheless, Oskar has a good opinion of him, remarking that "we are both heroes, quite distinct heroes." His hobby is to take the twine from gifts brought to Oskar and, knotting them, create figures that he then preserves by dipping into plaster. Bruno airs the room, runs errands, and narrates the chapter "Growth in a Freight Car" when Oskar's joints swell. His viewpoint puts the events into sober, simple perspective. In contrast to Oskar's style, he illuminates the difference between the simple narration of events and polished prose. Listening to Oskar's story, he feels neither uneasy nor puzzled but rather irritated that the narrative is often incoherent and not chronological. In short, Bruno is chiefly interested in Oskar only as a source of subject matter for his knotted figures.

ALBRECHT GREFF

The greengrocer across the street from Oskar's house is one of Grass' highly comic figures. In his business he emphasizes the aesthetic rather than the practical value of his merchandise, makes a religion of it, and becomes a vegetarian, thereby arousing the distrust of his stolid, carnivorous customers. He tries to make potato buying an aesthetic experience by attaching a gadget to the scales that plays folk songs at certain poundage. The aesthetic is defeated, however, when his efforts merely attract the suspicious attention of the Bureau of Weights and Measures.

A scoutmaster and author of a successful songbook, his interest in muscular young boys points to degeneracy. He enjoys bathing in the frozen Baltic in the dead of winter along with a nude frolic in the snow with his favorite scouts. These and similar eccentricities eventually result in a summons to appear in court on a morals charge. Greff's final victory over law and custom occurs when he commits suicide with the aid of potatoes which, when he is cut down, play a grotesque, cacophonous symphony.

LINA GREFF

Lina Greff is a foul-smelling slut who spends all day wallowing in a filthy bed. When Oskar is ejected from Maria's favors, he goes to Lina for comfort. This unhygienic affair is a ribald **parody** of contemporary events. While the German Army bogs down in the mud of Russia, Oskar roots about in Lina's slippery terrain. Finally, during the Russian occupation, Lina services legions of hungry soldiers, truly happy and content for the first time in her life.

KLEPP

"Klepp" is Oskar's nickname for his friend Egon Munzer ("Coiner"). His name is a pun on a real life friend of Grass, Geldmacher ("money maker"). Together with a third musician, the two, like Oskar, Klepp, and Scholle, formed a jazz trio in Dusseldorf after the war.

Klepp is an eccentric, sometime musician who lives in unbelievable squalor. His eccentricity allows him to admire the British royal family and the Communist Party at the same time and to see a relationship between jazz and Marxism. His life is characterized by inconsistency. While he has spent the last few months refusing to get out of bed, he allows Oskar's drum to rouse him from his lethargy to form a jazz group.

In this respect Klepp also functions as the modern Lazarus. In a way, his laziness and apathy can be regarded as a spiritual death. Oskar is able to raise him with his drum because he has learned how to reduce the joy of life to its rhythmical components. Following Oskar's solo, Klepp leaps from the bed, washes, and vows to begin life afresh.

ANNA KOLJAICZEK:

(pronounced: call-YAH-check) Slow of wit and low of brow, she is the family matriarch. It is from beneath her wide skirts that the Bronskis and finally Oskar himself emerge. For Oskar, she becomes the symbol of security and refuge, the gateway to the primary source of being. Not only does he regard her as the well-spring of all life but also the means by which he may reenter the womb. It is only beneath her skirts that he feels truly secure. From there he is able to view both his own life and current events in perspective. When he is homesick in Paris, he longs for her skirts; when he ascends the escalator that is to deliver him into the hands of the Interpol detective, he wishes that his grandmother stood there, large as a mountain, ready to take him under her skirts forever. As an independent **protagonist**, however, her role is small. Following the marriage of her daughter to Matzerath, she appears only at family reunions, holiday dinners, and at funerals. We hear nothing more of her after Oskar leaves for West Germany.

JOSEPH KOLJAICZEK

This figure represents the Polish side of Oskar's ancestry. Grass uses him to reflect the age old Polish-German conflict in all its ruthless inconclusiveness. Formerly a Polish partisan protesting the partition of Poland by burning down German sawmills, he decides to reform following his sojourn under Anna's skirts. But he is not permitted to live out his life in obscurity. Thirteen years later the police track him down. At the last moment he dives under the log raft and is drowned. Because his body is never found, several legends arise, one of which places him in Buffalo, New York.

LANKES

Callous, overbearing, and stingy, Lankes evaluates everything and everyone in terms of money. Although he smokes all day, he has never been known to buy a pack of cigarettes. While mooching cigarettes from his friends, he takes twenty pfennigs from one pocket and transfers it to another. After two years he is able to buy a piece of land with the money he has saved just from smoking.

His relationship with others is characterized by other people's cigarettes, selfishness, cruelty, and insensitivity. He slaps his girlfriend Ulla around the studio, orders her to model with Oskar, and takes the fees for himself. Then when she bores him, he flings her out into the street. He regards his art solely as a moneymaking proposition. It never occurs to him that one might express feelings through art, perhaps because he lacks feeling himself. Strangely, Lankes is unaware of his heartlessness; neither is he drawn to cruelty and bloodshed for its own sake. According to Grass, he is symbolic of the war criminal.

SCHUGGER LEO

After studying theology for several years, Schugger Leo one day underwent a spiritual transformation that resulted in a vision of pure and sublime happiness. Wishing to share the ecstasy with others, he turns up at every funeral in Danzig. Dressed in a shabby black suit and wearing mildewed, white gloves he waits, with an ecstatic smile and misty eyes, for the mourners to come out. Slavering profusely, he blubbers about how cheap things are in heaven, the benign weather, and the goodness of the Lord.

Schugger Leo is attuned to funerals in an uncanny way. No one in Danzig can pass away without his getting wind of it. When Jan Bronski is executed, Schugger Leo somehow hears about the funeral and turns up in time to note the exact spot of the unmarked grave and pick up a shell case left by the firing squad.

Despite his eccentricity, Schugger Leo is a person with powerful intuitions, well illustrated at Herbert Truckinski's funeral. When he approaches Meyn (the SA man) to proffer his condolences, he senses in him the diabolical and savage spirit of the Nazi Party. He convulsively jerks back his hand and runs screaming across the tombstones. Again at Matzerath's funeral, Schuger Leo is the first to notice that Oskar has commenced to grow and to recognize in him the new Messiah. Like Moses, who is only permitted a glimpse of the Promised Land, Schugger Leo is shot while proclaiming the news to the world.

AGNES MATZERATH

Oskar's mother is a portrait of the Danzig citizen of Cassubian peasant stock. Exposure to the cosmopolitan influence of the city stimulates a latent taste for little luxuries while her peasant ancestry accounts for her talent in retailing. This early division of her personality into two distinct, by no means compatible, parts defines the manner in which she organizes her life. First, she makes a practical choice in the matter of husbands, choosing the pragmatic Rhinelander Alfred Matzerath who likes to cook. Then she takes the suave Jan Bronski as her lover because he knows how to indulge her taste for the good things in life. On Thursdays and on Skat-playing evenings, she enjoys the role of mistress while during the rest of the week she is comfortable as the demure housewife, mother, and retailer. She is able to live the dual life as long as both the practical and passionate tendencies are kept in equilibrium.

This dual life, however, takes its toll when the passion for Jan Bronski grows out of proportion. The first indication that something is wrong occurs when she develops a yearning for sweet, fattening desserts. This is followed by her sudden interest in religion. Unable to differentiate between the symptoms and the causes of her spiritual malady, her condition worsens. She arranges matters so that she sees Bronski on Thursdays and then assures herself of six days of grace by going to confession on Saturday. This unhealthy arrangement overtakes her on the Good Friday outing to the seashore. After witnessing the loathsome way the longshoreman fishes for eels, Agnes develops a perverse taste for fish. In silent hysteria she consumes in the course of several weeks a lethal amount of fish. The author takes considerable pains to emphasize that the cause of her sickness and death lies in the unnatural division of her life into two parts.

ALFRED MATZERATH

Matzerath's most outstanding characteristic is that he has the power to metamorphosize feelings into soup. He is so attached to cooking that he endows food with feelings of its own. He slices, for instance, the Sunday roast with misty-eyed tenderness. Extroverted, loud, and naive, he becomes an early member of the Nazi Party simply because he likes to shout, sing, and applaud. As a result, he proves to be a conscientious party member and spends every Sunday at the parade grounds. Matzerath is also a kind and generous husband. During his wife's illness he takes care of her and is thoughtful and considerate. He is even prepared to adopt her unborn child as his own, although he knows it is probably not. At the Catholic funeral, the Protestant Matzerath is appealingly ill at ease, accepting with an awkward grin the shrieking vituperation that Grandmother Koljaiczek heaps upon him. Matzerath also proves to be a good father. He is genuinely sorry about his supposed fault in the accident that retarded Oskar's growth. And later when the authorities press him to commit Oskar to a health institution in the name of racial hygiene, he refuses, proclaiming loudly that he is Oskar's father and not the Board of Health. At this point Oskar is prepared to admit that Matzerath is his true father. Yet Oskar's malignant dislike of him results in Matzerath's death.

OSKAR MATZERATH

Oskar is born into the world with an adult's intelligence and wisdom. His attitude to life is reflected in his decision to stop growing at age three. By remaining three-feet tall and by pretending that he can neither speak nor comprehend, he is free of the necessity to conform to the adult world. Oskar rejects modern society as dehumanizing. He sees in its materialistic value-system something that crushes everything that is noble in man and keeps him permanently on a low level of development. The high premium placed on conformity and the arbitrary repression of primal urges either renders the individual neurotic or encourages unnatural sublimation. Oskar further rejects as unnatural the achievement-oriented social philosophy. Especially distasteful is the rapacious hedonism and frantic impulse to compete and to succeed. Oskar's chief complaint is that the individual is not permitted to equally develop all parts of his Self. While certain faculties and potentialities are declared evil and relegated to the Devil, others are recognized and encouraged. Since Oskar's primary concern is to develop all his talents, he must be free of all externally imposed moral systems. Thus, the reason for Oskar's decision not to grow becomes clear and rational.

Oskar fulfills an inner necessity to develop the evil aspects of his genius along with the good. Accordingly, he defines his character in terms of Rasputin and Goethe. While Rasputin stands for raw, untamed nature (the diabolical element in man), Goethe represents everything that is noble, beautiful, and sublime. His is the voice of reason and duty in preference to feeling and inclination. Since Oskar views himself as a combination of both good and evil, he is unable, and unwilling, to pass judgment on the inconsistencies, foibles, and weaknesses of those around him. His dual nature also accounts for a sometimes puzzling callousness. For instance, when he abandons the Dusters to their fate, causes Matzerath's death, and appears indifferent to Roswitha's death.

Endowed with these characteristics, Oskar emerges as the new Messiah. He believes that the traditional Christian Deity is inadequate for our times, for He represents only that half of the world that is good, pure, and noble. The other evil half, assigned to Satan, is denied. A truly representative religion, however, should sanctify the evil along with the good.

Perhaps because he is unsure of his ultimate fate, Oskar reluctantly accepts his role as the new Messiah. He would rather remain in the security of his hospital bed for the rest of his life. Thus Oskar ceases his narrative on a note of apparent indecision. While he pretends to consider several courses of action, it is clear that he will assume the role of Christ. For two years he has dreaded the day when he will be released from the hospital, for then he will be forced to gather disciples around him and face what he has brought upon himself.

MEYN

Meyn lives on the top floor of Oskar's apartment house, has four cats and, when he is not drunk (which is most of the time), plays the trumpet too beautifully for words. In this character Grass shows the corrupting effects of National Socialism on the individual. Infected with the Nazi fever, Meyn one days decides to turn over a new leaf. He gives up alcohol, joins the SA, and devotes his musical talents to playing military marches. The evil influence of Nazism is first reflected in Meyn's music. Whereas he formerly played his instrument beautifully, he has now lost the capacity to play with feeling. This loss reflects a salient feature of the Nazi ethical code that stressed the importance of acting only in accordance with duty and reason. Feeling and inclination as a basis for judgment was regarded as a sign of weakness.

Other Nazi principles are illuminated in the change of Meyn's character. The senseless murder of his four tomcats underscores the underlying barbarism of the movement and prefigures the officially sanctioned brutality and mass murder of the war years. These changes are brought out most clearly when the amazingly perceptive Schugger Leo looks into Meyn's soul and recoils in terror at what he sees there.

ROSWITHA RAGUNA

Compared to the other **protagonists** in the novel, the three midgets appear to be the only normal, well-adjusted individuals in the book. As if to compensate for their small stature, each is endowed with a specific power. Bebra foresees the future; Oskar possesses a glass-shattering voice; Roswitha has the power to look inside a person and see his inmost nature. Billed as Europe's greatest somnambulist, she surprises and often embarrasses soldiers by revealing their most private thoughts and desires. Roswitha is also the first person to see the strange mixture of Satanism and divinity in Oskar. Even though she is frightened by the diabolical in Oskar during their first meeting at the cafe, she later falls in love with him and becomes his mistress.

Roswitha's ancestry is left obscure (her name suggests Italian-German heritage) because she also functions as the symbol of woman. Her age is likewise a matter of conjecture. Eighteen or eighty, age old and eternal are some of the terms Oskar uses to suggest her age. She appears to have lived forever.

Perhaps Roswitha's most salient characteristic is her ability to live in complete harmony with herself and her environment. To her, the real world consists of the stage, hotel lounges, and cinemas. She lavishes childlike enthusiasm and becomes rapturous over little gifts, a bottle of wine, or a new city. When she speaks of Paris and describes her experiences there, she is carried away with a rapture as pure and genuine as that of a knowledgeable academe's ecstasy on discovering an unpublished letter by Goethe. She lives entirely in the present although she knows an uncertain future awaits her.

In her own way, she has remained aloof from bourgeois morality. Neither she nor Bebra think it strange that she loves both him and Oskar at the same time; nor is Bebra jealous. Furthermore, they do not hesitate to enjoy such delicacies as Russian caviar, Danish butter, and French wine while most of Europe is eating cabbage and potatoes.

HERBERT TRUCZINSKI

(pronounced: True-Chin-ski): Herbert does not function as an independent character but is used to illustrate Grass' views on the individual's relationship to politics and history. Big, uncomplicated, peaceful as well as friendly, he represents that vast apolitical majority of citizens who prefer peace to war and imagine themselves uninvolved in the course of events. Herbert works as a waiter in a waterfront tavern catering to an international clientele of low-brow seamen. Inevitably, the differing political ideologies lead to brawls and knife fights. Although Herbert is basically a peaceful man, he is drawn into the fisticuffs and thus symbolically drawn into politics. Grass is suggesting that nowadays the individual cannot avoid involvement in politics nor the responsibility for such involvement. The scars that Herbert carries on his back are the results of his unwilling participation. In Grass' view no one can disassociate himself from history. Willingly or not, every person is a part of history, and he bears equal responsibility for what happens in his age. In a way, he believes in a communal responsibility. One is born and is immediately responsible. This is well illustrated in the Niobe **episode**. Depressed at accidentally killing a man in a barroom brawl and seeking to disassociate himself completely from future involvement, Herbert takes a job as guard in the Maritime Museum. But even here he is slowly drawn into the historical process. Niobe tempts him to impersonate historical figures, to act out famous historical scenes, and finally to consummate his own death.

MARIA TRUCZINSKI

The most striking characteristic of Maria is that she has no outstanding one. After Agnes Matzerath dies, Albert hires her to work in the grocery store. She has a peasant's talent for retailing and soon catches on to the business. After a few months, Matzerath seduces her and, since he is not careful, is obliged to marry her. That she adjusts so well to her new life underscores the principle of social continuity. She steps into the life and role that Agnes vacated so well that after a short time it is as though Agnes had never existed.

Maria's singular lack of character and her undefined direction in life endow her with a great capacity to adjust to any situation. She adjusts her values to those of the Hitler era and is prepared to send Oskar to an extermination camp because the modern thing to do is purge the race of biological impurities. When Matzerath is shot by Russian soldiers, she gives no sign of grief and occupies herself with the practical results of his death. After Mr. Fajngold takes over the store in May, 1945, Maria makes herself at home in the potato cellar. Maria's willingness to organize her life according to current circumstances is most apparent in Dusseldorf. To support her family, she sells synthetic honey on the black market. Following the currency reform in 1948, she opens a delicatessen with Oskar's financial assistance. Now properly outraged at Nazi war crimes and genocide, she gravely shakes her head in authentic disbelief. But she, like many Germans, denies any responsibility for the past. Comfortable in her role as a successful businesswoman, she believes in the economic miracle; she takes seriously the posters depicting the Bolshevik with the knife between his teeth; she subscribes to fashion magazines.

Yet it is precisely Maria's ability to adapt that insured her survival in the critical period between 1944 and 1949. Both the economic miracle and the vitality of modern Germany rest in large part on such people.

ULLA

Called "The Muse" because of her ability to bring out the creative element in her artist friends, Ulla herself is devoid of talent or any other redeeming qualities. Although she regards her modeling as a genuine artistic creation, she is naive and empty headed. But she is attractive and she trades lovers like stamps, announcing before each new affair that she is finally embarking on a meaningful and lasting relationship. Ulla can be regarded as Grass' portrait of the modern muse. It is to such a person that the contemporary artist turns for inspiration.

GOTTFRIED VON VITTLAR

This figure is another of the author's incomplete protagonists. Vain, superficial, and bored with life, his one desire is to become famous. Oskar accommodates Vittlar by allowing him to accuse him of Sister Dorothea's murder. Vittlar's function in the novel, therefore, is to precipitate Oskar's trial and imprisonment in a mental institution.

THE TIN DRUM

ESSAY QUESTIONS AND ANSWERS

. . . .

Question: What are the characteristics of the Bildungsroman and how does Grass **parody** it?

Answer: The Bildungsroman, or Novel of Education, is primarily a German literary **genre** arising in the late eighteenth century. Characteristically, it follows the hero's development from the innocence of youth through a wide spectrum of cultural influence to the inner fulfillment and wisdom of maturity. The most salient example of this **genre** is Goethe's *Wilhelm Meister's Apprenticeship*. It is this novel that Grass parodies in *The Tin Drum*.

The **theme** of *Wilhelm Meister's Apprenticeship* can be quickly summed up. The son of a well-to-do merchant family, Wilhelm is fascinated with the stage. He revolts against the stifling bourgeois atmosphere at home and runs away with an actress. When he discovers that Marianne has been untrue to him, Wilhelm returns home and falls seriously ill. Later he joins another troupe of actors and spends several weeks at a Count's mansion rebuilding the troupe around himself.

The real change in Wilhelm's life occurs when he makes a short trip one day to upbraid a nobleman who has been acting in an ungentlemanly way with an actress. There he is introduced into a circle called "The Society of the Tower." The Society is a kind of ethical utopia in which people of distinctive character live according to a moral code held to be superior to the traditional Judeo-Christian system. He discovers that throughout his own life the Society has watched over his education from afar. He also finds a spiritual mentor in Jarno. Shortly after his arrival he discovers he has a child by Marianne and then marries her.

The Society teaches Wilhelm that the key to a meaningful existence lies in self-knowledge gained through activity within a community and the development of a specific talent. When Wilhelm understands this, he emerges from his apprenticeship. Thus the meaning of "Novel of Education" is defined. It is the story of the formation of the hero until he ceases to be self-centered and becomes society-centered.

Grass' **parody** of Goethe's novel begins in the first chapter when Oskar announces that he was born with an adult's intelligence and character. As a completely formed personality that needs only a certain amount of "filling in," the author negates the emphasis placed on character development.

Oskar's experience with the theater commences when he shatters the windows of the City Theater. This experience engenders an interest in the performing arts which he satisfies by attending Punch and Judy shows. His contact with legitimate theater takes place when he is taken to a performance of Wagner's *The Flying Dutchman*. After a few remarks about shrieking Teutonic sopranos, Oskar falls asleep.

The "Society of the Tower" is parodied when Oskar takes over the leadership of a gang of hoodlums called The Dusters. Under his direction, they decorate their headquarters with religious paraphernalia stolen from churches and organize their activities according to a vague ethical code that sets them against social involvement rather than for it.

Soon thereafter, Oskar is once again exposed to the theater as a member of a troupe of touring midgets. Oskar's excitement and involvement with perfecting his new glass-breaking acts bears close resemblance to Wilhelm Meister's absorption with Hamlet.

The midget Bebra is a **parody** of Wilhelm Meister's spiritual leader Jarno. Oskar refers to him as "my teacher and master" but the reader soon realizes that Bebra teaches him nothing.

The principle of maturation is parodied in Oskar's flight to West Germany after the war. Since his personality is already completed at birth, his growth is physical rather than spiritual in nature and takes the form of a grotesque metamorphosis. Even his maturation is achieved at the expense of youthful vitality in that his voice has lost its ability to break glass. Unlike the optimistic conclusion of Goethe's novel, *The Tin Drum* ends on a note of pessimistic uncertainty. Contrary to Goethe's view, Grass regards life as a meaningless, absurd activity. The optimism inherent in the Novel of Education is defeated when confronted by the viewpoint that human endeavor, life, and the development of all our potentialities is useless.

Question: Discuss the function of Oskar's drum.

Answer: Oskar's drum serves many different functions. It defines his relationship to the world, it is both a symbol of his individuality and a means of communication, and finally it serves as the organizing principle of his narrative.

As Oskar matures and learns more about the world his drum assumes a more involved function. In his early childhood, his attitude to people is determined primarily by their relationship to his drum. Oskar remembers his mother with love and affection because it was she who gave him his first instrument. Matzerath, on the other hand, is viewed at first with mistrust and then hatred because he wants to take away the drum.

Gradually Oskar's instrument becomes the symbol of his individuality and freedom. This is brought out most clearly during his first day at school. This highly symbolic **episode** depicts society's efforts to turn its youth into productive and useful citizens through the dismantling and re-assembling of the personality. Miss Spollenhauer, representing society, attempts to take away Oskar's drum, the symbol of his individuality. Her inability to do so signifies Oskar's willingness to sacrifice anything to preserve his individuality, even an education. Drums become so important to him that he is willing to sacrifice even Jan Bronski to get a new one. Oskar waits outside the Polish Post Office for several days and, although he is aware of the dangerous situation, prevails upon Jan to take him inside the building so that Kobyella can repair the drum. Oskar gets a new drum at the price of Jan's life. Throughout the novel, Oskar destroys drums at the same time he incurs responsibility for the deaths of several people. There is a definite thematic analogy between the destruction of drums and that of people. Nevertheless, Oskar's drum must not be viewed as a destructive principle. It is a constructive one. He uses it to look behind tribunes and church altars to ascertain the true nature of each institution and destroy that which seeks to regiment human nature.

The drum also serves as a receptacle for Oskar's guilt. When he periodically incurs responsibility for some malicious act, he is able to renew his innocence by transferring the guilt onto his drum. Significantly, when he buries the instrument in Matzerath's grave, he deprives himself of his means of atonement. Paradoxically, he merely exchanges one symbol for another, his drum for a hump. Oskar's grotesque metamorphosis into a misshapen dwarf signifies that one cannot escape guilt.

After the war, Oskar exchanges his drumsticks for a mallet and chisel with which he drums upon tombstones. Pounding meaningless **cliches** into granite, it is as if his own heart has become petrified, reflecting the horrors of the war and his responsibility in the deaths of four people. When he permits himself to feel again several years later, he acquires a new drum.

It is noteworthy that Oskar's acquisition of a new drum coincides with the German economic miracle. Here, the instrument takes on its chief function as a means of communication. Oskar's enormous success on his tours consists in his ability to awaken nostalgic memories of the past and to call up long-forgotten feelings. His audience mistakenly ascribes the delight of these memories to a magic quality in the drum. It is clear, however, that the drum has no such power. Oskar has merely learned how to reduce childhood experience, happiness, and fear to music and to communicate these feelings to his audience.

Finally, the drum serves as the organizing principle of his narrative. One day he discovers that memory is made up of a series of interconnected segments that assume their identity independent of chronological order. Furthermore, he learns that a physical sensation creates in the mind a connection between events widely separated in time. For example, when Oskar feels the patent-leather belt in Sister Dorothea's clothes closet, its texture reminds him of the shiny green eels on the breakwater which are in turn connected to his mother's illness and death. Oskar's drum functions in the same way as the patent-leather belt. Since the drum participates in Oskar's every experience, it serves as the agent linking all the disparate parts of his memory. Thus when he wishes to recall a past experience, he merely needs to drum the appropriate rhythm.

Question: What is Grass' view of history and how is it portrayed in *The Tin Drum*?

Answer: Many **metaphysical**, religious, and philosophical systems claim that man has an innate, fixed position in the universe. Such systems are based on the assumption that a specific formula, such as a certain way of life or of thinking, can be found that will enable us to understand the cosmos. Once a person has comprehended his position in the universe, he will understand with perfect clarity the meaning of his existence and his purpose in the whole scheme of things. Through this knowledge he will experience a pure and perfect happiness. Other thinkers view history as a coherent, comprehensible chain of events. Still others believe that history is a force possessed of an ultimate purpose and that it is slowly progressing toward a Golden Age in which universal harmony will prevail. Grass rejects such systems as unrealistic. His philosophy of history reflects his view of life. He believes that man is an insignificant creature living in a world without meaning or unifying principle. Man's religions, philosophy, and even his science are evidence of his efforts to impose meaning where there is none. Grass illustrates his viewpoint in several ways, chiefly through **parody**. Parody is an effective way of reflecting his pessimistic views because it trivializes. This is brought out in the scene in which the glorious U-Boat victories are announced while

Matzerath and Maria fornicate on the sofa. In fact, all historical events are played out against a background of uncouth, frequently repelling, proletarian biography. The Treaty of Rapallo is parodied in that Agnes both marries Matzerath and commits adultery on this date.

Grass' philosophy of history functions in the assumption that man is inextricably involved in the historical process and that the individual cannot avoid the responsibility for such involvement. Another feature of Grass' view of history claims that the individual has little if any influence on the course of events. Even such a figure as Adolf Hitler is seen as insignificant. After Danzig falls to the German Army in September, 1939, the author conveys Hitler's unimportance by placing his name at the end of a long participial phrase.

Grass describes recent history by analogy and **metaphor** because it is next to impossible, he feels, to convey through words the terror of events that many readers experienced firsthand. Accordingly, the spectacle of Polish cavalry attacking the German armored divisions and the ensuing slaughter is rendered by describing a spectacular sunset to which the dying squadrons add another dash of red.

The effect of current events on the people is kept in the background. The growing scarcity of food toward the end of the war is conveyed by noting parenthetically the increase in the number of rabbits raised in the courtyard. The movement of vast numbers of troops to the Eastern front makes it difficult for citizens to travel by train, and such names as Monte Casino and Stalingrad appear.

A final device that Grass employs with particular effectiveness is that of relating events in the form of a fairy tale. In the chapter "Faith, Hope, Love," which describes the Nazi attacks on Jewish places of business, each segment is preceded by the traditional fairy tale opening "once upon a time" and ends with "and if they aren't dead, they're still alive." This technique enables the author to accurately describe the cruelty of that evening without becoming lost in statistics and moralizing.

THE TIN DRUM

. . . .

THEMES OF *THE TIN DRUM*

Validity of Grass' Social Criticism
The Drum as a Means of Communication
The Tin Drum and Modern Germany
Nature of Guilt in *The Tin Drum*
Nature of Suffering in *The Tin Drum*
Oskar's Relationship to Women
Religion and Atheism in *The Tin Drum*
Psychology of C. G. Jung in *The Tin Drum*
Nazism as a Force for Evil in *The Tin Drum*

HISTORICAL BACKGROUND

Grass' Philosophy of History
Portrayal of History and Contemporary Events in *The Tin Drum*

Historical Events and Their Influence on the Individual
Grass' View of the Economic Miracle and Post-War Germany

GRASS' CHARACTERIZATION

Grass' Portrayal of Women
Lobsack and National Socialism
Meyn and National Socialism
Herbert Truczinski and the European Common Man
Anna Koljaiczek and the Theme of Security
Fizz-Powder and Coca-Cola as Historical Characterization
Corporal Lankes as a War Criminal
The Polish-German Conflict and its Role in Characterization

OSKAR

Oskar as a Christ Figure
Oskar as an Existentialist
Oskar as Everyman
Grass' Oskar and Heller's Yossarian
Oskar: Anti-Hero or New Hero?
Fictional Transformation of Jesus: Hermann Hesse's Demian and Günter
Grass' Oskar Matzerath
Oskar as the Modern Odysseus

GRASS' TECHNIQUES

Skat as a Technique of Characterization

The Tin Drum and the Theater of the Absurd

First and Third Person Narrative as an Alienation Technique

Satire and Parody: Grass' Two Modes

Grass' Metaphors and Their Literary and Psychological Impact

Grass' Puns: What Do They Add to Theme and Characterization?

Object-Metaphor in *The Tin Drum*

The Tin Drum and the novel of the Absurd

Symbolism of Odors and Colors in *The Tin Drum*

COMPARISONS WITH OTHER WORKS, OTHER WRITERS

Goethe's *Wilhelm Meister* and Grass' *The Tin Drum*: A Comparative Study

Bertolt Brecht and Günter Grass: Technique of Alienation

Extended Metaphor in Franz Kafka and Günter Grass

Organization of Experience in Marcel Proust and Günter Grass

The Tin Drum and Doblin's *Berlin*: Alexanderplatz: A Comparison in

Theme and Impact

Anxiety in the Fiction of Kafka and Grass

The Tin Drum and the Picaresque Novel

CHRONOLOGICAL TABLE OF GRASS' MAIN WORKS

1958 *Only Ten Minutes to Buffalo*

1959 *The Tin Drum*

1961 *Cat and Mouse, The Wicked Cooks*

1963 *Dog Years, Flood*

1965 *Mister, Mister*

1966 *The Plebians Rehearse the Uprising*

1969 *Local Anaesthetic*

1972 *From the Diary of a Snail*

BIBLIOGRAPHY

Bance, A. F. "The Enigma of Oskar in Grass's Blechtrommel," *Seminar*, III (Fall 1967), 147–156. Good textual analysis. Sees Oskar as one of the archetypes of Western fiction.

Boa, Elizabeth. "Günter Grass and the German Gremlin," *German Life and Letters*, 23 (1970), 144–151. The author examines Oskar's role as protagonist and considers the attitude of Oskar the narrator.

Cunliffe, W.G. "Aspects of the Absurd in Günter Grass," *Wisconsin Studies in Contemporary Literature*, VII, No. 3 (1966), 311–327. This study investigates Grass' use of the absurd as a literary technique. An excellent analysis.

———————— *Günter Grass* (New York, 1969). The most complete study of Grass to date. Scholarly, essential.

Enzensberger, Hans Magnus. *Einzelheiten* (Frankfurt, 1962), p. 221–233. Puts Grass into perspective. Some good insights.

Friedrichsmeyer, Erhard. "Aspects of Myth, **Parody**, and Obscenity in Grass' Die Blechtrommel and Katz und Maus,'" *Germanic Review*, XL (1965), 240–247. Investigates *The Tin Drum* in terms of Jungian psychology.

Hatfied, Henry. "Günter Grass: The Artist as Satirist," *The Contemporary Novel in German: A Symposium*. (Austin, 1967), p. 115–134. Discusses Grass' use of satire.

Maurer, Robert. "The End of Innocence: Günter Grass' *The Tin Drum*," *Bucknell Review*, 16 (1969), 45–65. This is a careful study of Oskar's progress from innocence to awareness and the incurring of guilt.

Scharfman, William L. "The Organization of Experience in *The Tin Drum*," *Minnesota Review*, VI (1966), 59–66. This article investigates Grass' method of literary construction.

Tank, Kurth Lothar. *Günter Grass* (Berlin: Colloquium Verlag, 1965). A complete and excellent study of Grass.

Van Abbe, Derek. "Metamorphosis of Unbewaltigte Vergangenheit in Die Blechtrommel," *German Life and Letters*, 23 (1970), 152–160. This article investigates how the Germans and particularly Grass have dealt with Nazism in their literature.

Wagenbach, Klaus. "Günter Grass," *Schriftsteller der Gegenwart: 53 Portrats*, ed. Klaus Nonnemann (Olten and Freiburg, 1963), p. 118–126. A short but good analysis.

Wilson, Leslie A. "The Grotesque Everyman in Günter Grass's Die Blechtrommel," *Monatshefte*, 58, (1966), 131–138. A thorough and penetrating analysis of several main themes.